for she has *holy fire* in her veins

A Faith Over Fear Novel

JORDAN NOELLÉ FINLEY

10 9 8 7 6 5 4 3 2 1
Library of Congress Cataloging-in-Publication Data is available.

ISBN 979-8-89041-975-0
ISBN 979-8-89041-976-7 (ebook)

FOR SHE HAS FIRE
IN HER VEINS

What drives our powerful women of today? Do you ever sit and ponder our ancestors? Wonder how they survived those harrowing voyages on the unruly open sea or the rugged, wild western terrains?

It seems unfathomable that people lived without electricity or roads that paved the way.

What fueled the young Prairie girl and the southern sharecropping child to be able to lead oxen to plow grounds for miles? To work tirelessly in the fields raising animals, growing fruit, vegetables, and fresh whole grains?

It had to be the holy fire running in her veins.

That holy fire must be hereditary and passed down from generation to generation.

What makes me ponder on the pioneering woman's strength from yesterday?

If only we could somehow encapsulate their power and inject their strength into the women of this day and age.

The courage of Rosa Parks' steadfastness and the brawns of Laura Ingalls Wilder need to be implanted into the women of today so that their holy fire can ignite the causes we fought for from slipping into obscurity.

That vivaciousness that once compelled suffragists with absolutely no legal rights to boldly and eloquently write out their pleas for equality and today's popular culture is simply not there.

Today, it's considered "empowering" for a woman to opt for vulgar self-expression and to expose her body in provocative wear.

No one is suggesting that women in the twenty-first century live as if they were in the Victorian era in order to exude dignity.

Yet rather to uphold the intellectualism that the Trail Blazers before us fought for in the first, second, and third wave of women's liberation, a cause that women are still fighting for to this day.

The image of a woman bearing her breasts in the heyday of the 1970s was a supremely liberating portrayal of the dominant freedom that women possess over their sexuality, bodies, and lives. Whereas a decade prior, a woman needed her husband's written permission to even procure employment, this was an astonishing achievement.

The holiness is missing from modern day feminism today for women. Sexual freedom is only as liberating to the woman as a woman is liberated financially.

For example, if the same seductive and sultry lyrics were sung by a destitute woman living at the haven of rest versus a rich woman driving in a Bentley, the entire meaning is night and day and now becomes toxic. The song is only an anthem of empowerment if the woman is considered wealthy, which sends a message that only a rich woman can be sexually freed, and the poor woman can't participate as she will be viewed as promoting prostitution, an archaic regression to female slavery.

If the song cannot be sung by and empower all women of every race, age, and demographic, feminism falls flat and caters to misogynistic attitudes cloaked in women's liberty.

So, what inspires the modern-day feminist to stare down the sexually explicit culture and brand of femininity?

To challenge and expose its own hypocrisy directly in its face?

It is she who does not forget the lessons that she learned from her predecessors before her; it is she who finds a rising confidence in herself, knowing that she walks with the strength of her ancestors within her, for she has holy fire in her veins.

TABLE OF CONTENTS

INTRODUCTION

This is a story about how a crushing loss in faith due to an unforeseen loss led to a trial that gave me the will to live again and overcome it with Jesus Christ's Scripture as my anchor. The story of Faith and I includes my growing pains with life without her and the lifelong lessons I learned along the way, with mishaps that drew me closer to God, amazing accomplishments, and influencing law reform in foster care settings in the state of Ohio.

I'm also writing this book on my identical twin sister Faith's homicide and our lives before it, how our journey to foster care for two years changed our lives, a law in the state of Ohio banning face-down restraints referenced as the "Faith Finley Law." About a young girl's courage to stand up for herself and for others and how she has impacted other people's lives. How God helped me overcome the shock of suffering and even learn from my own mistakes along the way.

As twins, we could feel each other. My twin and I truly were identical twins. But now, with life without her as a Twinless Twins Support Group Intl.™ I understand that sibling rivalry or Caine and Ableism start from birth or conception once life consciousness begins. My mom told me Faith and I had sibling rival fights she saw on the sonogram in the womb! I'm also writing this for families to know that kids in foster care are special, even if they have family issues, and not to count them out. Foster care kids can overcome family rifts, trauma, and the shock of suffering and come back stronger, more resilient, and more successful than ever.

CHAPTER 1:

The Day "My Faith" in Life Was Momentarily Crushed

The day my faith in life was temporarily crushed didn't happen in the literal sense that you might imagine. No belligerent bully came shouting, proclaiming, "I'll kill your faith in humanity, you weakling!" Instead, it happened on a grey and rainy morning and materialized in the form of a thin-lipped old man's emotionless, monotone voice and cold eyes staring into a seventeen-year-old girl's bewildered brown eyes.

Only my faith in humanity — and my belief that one day everything was going to be all right — was wrapped up in a person who I loved even more than I loved the inspiring community and idealism that the church provided.

My faith was my twin sister, Faith Finley.

And the crushing and emotionless voice telling me that my faith, my sister, was dead was the ever-present Mr. Dave, the in-house counselor of my teen group home I was to be in until I turned eighteen.

"Please sit down," he said and ushered me into his office, where brown wood chairs and tables and odd trinkets he'd collected moved about or glared inquisitively.

The formality of being invited into his office as if it were some great honor or adventure always slightly annoyed me, as if the trip from the living room to his office was some big journey for the kids forced to be in the limitations of STC or the Secured Treatment Center.

It felt more like a prison than a place to help "troubled" kids with mental health issues stemming from physical or emotional abuse.

His somewhat-warm demeanor immediately put me on edge because Mr. Dave was not known to be an affectionate therapist. His approach to mental health was to robotically tell kids that our parents were inadequate and that we were sent here to relearn what our parents had failed at teaching us.

I liked Mrs. Cynthia better; she would talk to any of us one-on-one if we asked her and treated each of our stories as fascinating and completely unique from each other, not lumping us all into a category of forgotten toys like the others did.

"I've been on the phone with the facility your sister was at Parmadale since 5 a.m. Did you know that your sister tried to go AWOL a few weeks ago?" He rubbed his temples and adjusted his glasses as if the mere act of talking about my sister exhausted him. How dare he be so cavalier about my beautiful Faith?

"No, of course not. You never tell me anything about her when I ask."

"Because you're not in the open cottages like she was; you're here for self-harm and being a threat to yourself and others!" he barked; the nice persona was gone.

I could feel my blood already starting to boil at his uncaring harshness, him holding my whole life in his hands and doing so callously.

"What do you mean 'like she was'? She's still there, isn't she?" I couldn't help my voice screeching a little at this point, to my dismay. I had vowed to be stone-cold throughout this whole experience; I'd planned it out in my head. We'd go in foster care for two years, from sixteen to eighteen. Once we aged out, we could use resources that "underprivileged kids" get and get an apartment together and start college together at Kent State, just like we'd always planned.

"As I was saying before your little outburst, did you know that your sister tried to go AWOL by jumping out of a two-story building and broke her arm?"

"Why didn't you tell me?" I cried, my breathing starting to increase as I could tell he was building up to something.

"Would that have done anything for your treatment? Stop interrupting me if you want to know what happened to your sister!"

"But is she in the hospital? Can I go visit her?"

"No!" He exhaled deeply and paused for a moment. "Your sister is dead. They just told me this morning. Your mother has been on the phone screaming at me since 4 a.m., and I don't even have all of the information."

His voice started to fade out, and I could feel cold sweat on my shoulders, my face heating, and my heart sinking.

"But she just came to visit me a couple of weeks ago; she was fine. She told me the ladies there spoiled her, braided her hair, and called her their daughter. She even got special privileges because she was good at getting the younger kids to listen. She told me that she had started going to Catholic church — even though we were raised Baptist, she was getting closer to God, she told me. She told me to stay strong and stop cutting so we could get released sooner. And you're telling me she's dead! *Dead?* My sister isn't dead; she was just right here! What is your problem? You always want everything to be bad for everyone here — please let me call my mom now!"

"Your mother is on her way up here from Akron. She and a family friend and…" He hurriedly flipped note pages. "…And she's trying to get your grandmother to come up from Warren, she says, in between all of the profanity and yelling — wait, where are you going?"

His voice began fading and echoing. I don't know why, but it felt like someone had punched me in the chest. I walked the hallways leading to the classroom and lunchroom, where the large windows fogged but showed the outside world to us, the snow falling down, where I'd sometimes sit to feel the draft slipping in, to feel like I was closer to the world than to this stupid, depressing place.

I leaned against it and felt my knees buckle; I pressed my hand against the cold windowpane and felt my legs giving out when Mrs. Cynthia came over to hold me while beckoning someone else to help her.

Shrill screams came out of my gaping lips. I couldn't close them; I couldn't stop them. That scared me, and it wouldn't stop. I clutched my swollen arm, still healing, to try and ooze more blood from it, but nothing but crying out to God could distract me from this kind of pain. The emotional pain was overbearing. This place started to feel not only like jail but like a monstrous pit that I had thrown us in and that had swallowed my last bit of hope and freedom along with it.

My faith was dead. They had killed my faith. And it was all my fault. Even if it wasn't directly my fault, at the time, I couldn't shake the feeling until I grew up. I felt a heavy spirit come upon me with the hugs from Mrs. Cynthia.

I cried out to God, "Lord, my heart hurts! Oh, be a rock for me! In Jesus' name, I pray. Amen and amen!"

> *The LORD is close to the brokenhearted and saves those who are crushed in spirit.*
>
> — Psalm 34:18 (NIV)

I can't exactly remember what happened next. I think I was probably carried to my room by a small group of staff members. When I finally awoke, I noticed that the whole day had been changed from the usual schedule. The kids were now segregated strictly to the classroom and lunchroom, and it was barricaded off by the medicine carts to prevent me from entering or to show me that I wasn't supposed to go there. I had to presume that I passed out because I remember being in my bed in pitch-black darkness, then waking up and getting up. Maybe it was just a bad dream. I got up and went to the common area/living room, but no one was there.

That wasn't right because if I was out here, then all the kids would be out here too; we moved through the facility like a unit.

I sat on the floor in a daze for a while until I heard clamoring at the metal door, and someone being buzzed in the secured door. I heard the jingling of keys and Mr. Dave's voice letting someone in and talking to the two staffers, Mr. Adam and Mr. Julius. Then it started coming back to me. While I was in the hallway, all four staff members surrounded me as I cried out on the floor, and then Mr. Adam sprinted into action, saying, "The kids have to be put in the classroom; the whole day can't stop because this has happened."

So, it wasn't a dream. Or a nightmare. This was real. All too real. A staff member instructed me to go to my room and pack because my aunt was on her way from Warren to pick me up. I went to my room, and the bright fluorescent lights hurt my eyes. I looked at the photos I had of Faith and me that she had printed out from our MySpace page and some new ones she had taken while at Parmadale. One of Macy and Spike, our beloved beagle girl and noble fox terrier boy pets. I felt like a ball of fire in my chest was being stoked and soon blazing into a flame of hatred. I started ripping the photos off the walls and screaming at the staff watching me pack, "You killed my twin sister! You're evil monsters! I can feel her with me. She's still alive, I know it! I feel her more than I thought I ever have!"

Mrs. Cynthia and another lady came to console me, but I started throwing clothes at them.

"Get out! Get away from me! I swear, you don't care! Get away from me!" I cried. Every scream felt like a leaf of dignity was falling away, making my face burn hot with embarrassment, but I didn't care. I wanted to die. More than I ever had before. I screamed for hours. Until my ears hurt. Until my throat was raw. "Jesus, just take me home so I can be with her!" "Jesus, God, I can't take this pain; carry it for me!" "Jesus, be a rock for me; I need Your help!" "Jesus, help me make something of myself!" all night long. I realized my prayer was what carried me through.

In Retrospect, How God Helped Me Defeat Anxiety

We are hard pressed on every side, but not crushed; perplexed, but not in despair; persecuted, but not abandoned; struck down, but not destroyed.

— 2 Corinthians 4:8–9

I had to get honest with the Lord in my new diary by speaking to Him as if I could truly cast all my cares upon Him because He cares for me.

I started with, "I'll be honest with You, Lord. I don't know how my despair could possibly drive someone closer to You. Before I came to this evolvement of my faith in God through persecution, whether by Your own hand or Satan's attacks borne out of hatred of Your chosen people and demonic thirst for blood or borne out of my own rebellion and reckless decisions, God, I realize You can even use my mistakes to create a deeper need for Your Holy Spirit."

I had to be honest with God and myself that I felt like I deserved rebellion due to being betrayed by Faith's homicide, unfairly teased and discriminated against when I was younger, that those crushing fates owed me reckless abandon due to past injuries... I was overwhelmed. It wasn't until re-reading the Bible and the story of Elijah, a mighty prophet during a turbulent time in Israel's history. The nation had turned away from the Lord to worship Baal, and King Ahab had formed an alliance with Sidon by marrying their princess, Jezebel. Elijah was sent to show Israel the evil of their ways and encourage them to return to the Lord.

Elijah wasn't awarded some magical reckless abandonment because he faced many trials; comparatively, only the prodigal son gave in to his temptation to sin. Jesus tells the well-known parable of the prodigal son, who asks his father for his inheritance, and then squanders it recklessly as he lives a life of indulgence. With nothing left of his fortune, he is forced to work as a hired hand for a pig farmer.

I had to be honest with myself about which one I was more like. In my most rebellious stages, I was definitely more of a fleeting Elijah who leaned heavily toward the haven of the prodigal son's recklessness, always hoping to run back to God's never-ending forgiveness, never taking into account that even Christ's patience with my grief would run out. I had to be honest with myself that I, too, had become like the world I was always running to, the nightclubs, parties, and bars, and that bad company truly does corrupt good character (1 Corinthians 15:33). I had to acknowledge and accept that I wasn't as sanctified as my monthly church visit in the world's eyes would have me liked to believe.

Acknowledging that I, too, had become bloodthirsty and that my holy fire from the Holy Spirit had become a ball of rage in my chest and face and was exploding into balls of fists, profanities, and a need or desire to break something... or someone. Then how could I ever get free from that rage and help heal another if I never gave my anger to the foot of the cross?

How could another boy or girl reading my sister's story ever think they could be truly set free from the prison of anger? If I didn't release my anger, I realized I wouldn't ever help someone else be free. Someone who was like me and had "momentarily" stopped clinging to their faith. Like the woman with the issue of blood clung to the hem of Jesus' garment so that she may be healed.

I'm here to tell you that the sweet day you have been waiting for, to be free from rage, anxiety, and despair, is here right now.

Not "one day" because you're a blessing right now. "Let us not become weary in doing good, for at the proper time we will reap a harvest if we do not give up" (Galatians 6:9, NIV).

Our hearts will be free from the pain of spiritual warfare in Jesus' name!

I placed my hand on my heart, prayed, and wrote:

Jesus, take this heart worn from battling blood-sucking spirits. Lord, take this heart so full of character and talent and kindness, made in Your image; make this heart just like Yours, Father God. Lord, take this heart and make it as strong as Yours. Lord, take this heart and make it strong enough to withstand the daggers sunk into it like the sword of betrayal, the jab of a pretending spirit, the wound of abandonment, the dagger of deceit, the blade of heartbrokenness and diabolical attacks, and the sword of caste systems that control the value of my life.

Lord, make my heart like Yours that is brave enough to hold enough courage to leave a small vein open for love *to seep in. Lord, give me a heart like Yours. Your heart is brave!*

I receive Your peace that passes all understanding right now, in the name of Jesus. I thank You, Jesus. Amen. Your heart was designed by God to be used for His supernatural kingdom. Your newly healed heart was made to act as the hands and feet of a loving yet kind, bold yet meek, awesome God.

A God who exalts the good qualities about me before all of the mistakes and makes those qualities live on in our minds, in our hearts, and in our souls.

A God who exalts the love for a family, exalts the joy of working an honest day's labor. A God that manifested into human form and separate entity in the Holy Trinity, in His Son, Jesus Christ.

A God that stood in the face of fear without giving in but with righteous indignation. A God who empowers what is low to shame the high. "But God chose what is foolish in the world to shame the wise; God chose what is weak in the world to shame the strong" (1 Corinthians 1:27-31 NIV).

That God is a God worth fighting for. Not only fighting for Him but fighting on His side.

A God that's always there for us. Twenty-four seven. Nights and weekends.

We can always "cast all your anxiety on him because he cares for you" (1 Peter 5:7, NIV).

In not abusing His life-saving grace set upon our lives. We must vow in our hearts to immediately repent if we feel ourselves desiring those quick magic tricks. Help us, God, to remember that magic quick fixes are almost always those blades and daggers from the wolves in sheep's clothing in our lives.

Help us, God, to remember that hatred only repays you with betrayal. Heart-wrenching. Nothing more. Thank You for always healing our hearts, Lord. In Jesus' name, amen and amen.

As I was praying and rocking all night long, clutching my photos and clothes in a heap on the floor, I heard Mr. Dave saying, "Leave her alone; Jordan can resume her classwork after she visits with her mother," and the staff left.

They came back with a syringe because I wouldn't stop — couldn't stop — screaming and crying out for my sister. My other half. The one I had been in the womb with. The syringe immediately took me out, and I was asleep for a while.

When I awoke, I could see even from the heavily grated windows that the day was fading into evening, and my throat was so sore that I couldn't talk when I tried. I got out of bed, opened the door, and saw the kids were back. Some were quietly drawing while others talked and murmured quietly amongst themselves, staring at me.

A nice blonde-haired staff lady who was the sister of Mr. Adam came over to me and said, "Some of the kids have decided to draw you some pictures and condolence cards. It was their idea."

There, I saw about four or five girls and one or two of the younger boys drawing rainbows on colorful card letters; one young brunette girl came over to me slowly as I sat down.

"Here's mine; I drew a picture of you and your sister as an angel and holding hands, too. We all feel so bad..." She handed me her drawing, and I couldn't see it because my eyes were blurring with tears.

One by one, they handed me various pictures they'd drawn and notes they'd written on them, and a pile started building.

"Thank you," I said in a cracked voice I didn't recognize. I swallowed and tasted a strange acidic blood. Unbeknownst to me, that was the start of a throat ulcer from the nerves bursting in my mouth.

The days blurred together, and with the sedation, I don't remember when, but eventually, my mom showed up. The snow was falling heavily, and I was worried about her being out there on the roads by herself; even if we were estranged now, we hadn't always been. I had helped take care of her with her fibromyalgia or joint pain illness for as long as I can remember.

Our curfew was ten, but because she called and said she was almost there, the staff let me wait for her in the cafeteria. Through the foggy windows I saw headlights slowing pulling in, then I heard her familiar rattle of keys and smelled her signature "Knowing" Estée Lauder perfume and knew she was here. She had visited me somewhat regularly as she saw that my hair was breaking off, partially from stress and mostly from the fact that I wasn't allowed my silk head scarf as it was seen as a "potential threat" or something I could harm myself with. She would visit and insist on moisturizing and nurturing my hair; she always helped deep condition my hair back at home.

This time, she came to visit for an entirely different reason. When she was finally allowed in the room, I remember falling into her arms and holding onto her for a long time. I rested my head in her familiar bosom; she was always so warm and cuddly when I hugged her that for a minute, I closed my eyes, and it was as if I wasn't there and we were back home in Barberton during our good days, and Spike and Macy were playing around on the floor, Faith was practicing her flute and my mom and I were hugging while she made one of her famous delicious dishes after a long day at work.

I opened my eyes to the harsh fluorescent light and remembered that I wasn't there at all. Mommy's eyes looked tired and wet, and she had one of the silk blouses I used to wash and set out for her after doing the chores. Anything I could do to help as she managed the bourgeoning weight of caring for us without our stepdad on her fatigued shoulders.

We stood there for a long time, and Mr. Julius told us, "Take your time," and quietly exited, even though I knew he didn't have control over how long my mom could stay.

"Oh, baby. I know." She exhaled sharply. "Oh, little girl, little girl. Be a big, strong girl and sit with me."

For a minute, I sat on her lap, afraid to leave her that if I didn't cling to her, she would disappear. She explained to me that Mr. Dave had called her early that morning and told her about Faith trying to go AWOL with some girls and having a cast put on her arm a few weeks back.

"Why didn't you tell me?" I asked weakly, with what felt like everything in me not to pass out right there in front of my mom.

"I only thought it'd worry you unnecessarily…" she trailed off. I know a part of her felt conflicted with our being there, wrongfully villainized for simply being a poor and struggling single mother. "If I had never called those so-called counselors to come talk to you, this would've never happened," she began.

"Well, you did, and you were just trying to help us. Help Faith and me. You were too overprotective and controlling of us, yes, but you weren't a monster."

Her eyes started to water, and she batted them with a soiled napkin she had been clutching since she walked in.

"Thank you, baby. I know I wasn't perfect by any stretch of the imagination, but like I said before, if I had brought you in here with rug burn marks on your face the way these people have, I'd be in jail."

"Well, also, I probably wouldn't have been restrained so harshly or even sent here if I wasn't cutting," I reminded her.

She scoffed solemnly. "Yeah. More punishment for being a child who's suffering from trauma. They should've kept you in the hospital like I requested... but of course, they wouldn't listen."

"How did she die? Did they tell you?"

"They say she was throwing a fit and that they were forced to restrain her... they wouldn't give her back her Walkman, and they said she started screaming and cursing at them."

"They?"

"It was three women altogether. That one enormous 300-pound lady we saw with Faith at that one McDonald's the last time we were all together. When Faith said she would never speak to me again after all this." A small level of disdain entered her voice as she recollected.

"Please don't get caught up on that; how could she die from a restraint?"

"You saw that one girl. What was her name?"

"Denise."

"Yes, Denise. That one day, I came to visit, and we heard her being thrown down into a restraint, and she was screaming she was hurt, but they wouldn't get off of her."

"They broke her collar bone."

"Yes… well, we still have to wait for the coroner's report to come back, but they're saying that there was internal bleeding and…"

My heart felt like it was gurgling inside my chest. "No," I started, but Mommy finished.

"And her best friend Temika heard her screaming that she said she couldn't breathe, but they wouldn't stop!" My mom's voice started to shrill, and a swift knock came at the door.

"Mrs. Finley, they're saying it's getting late and that you'll have to come back tomorrow," Mr. Julius said woefully.

"Okay. One more thing," my mom said, sniffling and gathering her things. "Remember that nice lady Jill you met right before you switched places? Anyways, she's agreed to work on our case pro bono. We're going to sue Parmadale, and we won't stop until those demons are behind bars."

"Good," I said. "And Mommy. Please don't fall into a depression right now and disappear. I need you. I really need you right now…" I trailed off, swallowing back tears building in my throat, trying to breathe slowly, praying in my head that I wouldn't faint from the pressure of facing death.

"You know it's funny I met your stepdad at the library at Kent State," my mom would say in retrospect. She would jokingly add, "Him singing that silly 'play that funky music white boy' song to me on our first date. Even though he was Russian. Heh, maybe that's why he's so dang 'on crazy. Boy of boy, little babies. If only I just would have picked up that book at the top shelf by myself instead of letting him get it for me. I could've spared you and Faithy a world of undeserved pain."

"Mrs. Finley, I'm getting the signal," Mr. Julius said, making a windmill motion with his hand, still holding the door half open."

"That's okay then," she said, gathering her purse and papers. "Your aunt Ella will be here in the morning, and we're getting you out of this hell hole as soon as possible, baby."

I clung to her side one last time as we descended down the long hallway. I was so scared that she'd get into an accident on the way home, but she told me friends had put her up in a hotel and to not worry about her. I walked with her until I was led back to the common area and sat there until I saw her headlights turned on and was given a trazodone pill to sleep.

Many are the afflictions of the righteous: but the LORD delivereth him out of them all.

— Psalm 34:19 (KJV)

CHAPTER 2 :

Calm before the Storm

Much before life in STC, life was in Barberton. My mom, Antio-nette, found herself a recently divorced twenty-something from choir boy Andrew Finley, my biological father. She was fleeing from his secret abuse in their flat in Chicago with two twin infants, my sister Faith and me.

She fled back to her hometown in Warren, Ohio, at the safety of Granny's. Before Toni met John, we lived in Warren with Grandma Idella and Grandad, who settled there from Alabama with her daughter, my nana Carol, for some time. There we settled back into stability and enjoyed growing tall sunflowers and vegetables with Granny in the garden. Mommy had even decided to go back to college.

"Now, with gardening, baby, there's a few things you need to know. Mostly, don't be scared of a little mud! You have to get your hands real deep in the soil, like this," Granny said jubilantly and matter-of-factly, putting her soft hands in the flower bed, churning the soft dirt up to her elbows.

"Granny, wait. Look! There's a snake right there! Will it bite us?" A four-year-old me gasped, but Granny held my hand in hers, making my hand shoe the little amphibian out of the way.

"Oh, baby, that ain't nothin' but a garter snake, nothing to be afraid of. You always remember that, ya hear? Jesus tells us to not be afraid."

"Yes, Granny," I said, watching the sun twinkle through her hair, in awe at her beauty and abilities.

I got saved at my uncle George's church that same year at four years old at church with my mom and Faithy. I just remember a warm feeling coming over me when I said the word Jesus. I felt the Holy Spirit for the first time and felt a bright light beaming down on me that I will never forget. Looking up at my mother's face beaming with tearful joy, and my uncle's resounding voice and strong hand at my back, guiding me through this moment of salvation. That experience brought awareness about the good and bad sides to life, dark and light, of the sun and the moon, but that God created all of it, and He can still show lights in dark places.

Years later in Barberton, before our family would split up for good, my mother again found herself recently divorced, with two twin tweens by her side. She decided to start working two, sometimes three, jobs at a time: one as a night shift manager at Sheetz, then in a factory called Luke in Wooster (though the heavy labor proved too much for her). And eventually as a home health aide for MRDD patients or high-functioning adults with disabilities. All these jobs and the different cities we were constantly moving to were in the attempt to escape from her husband, my stepfather, John Maksimovich. A man she had once loved and married and trusted.

To think of the woman my mom once was, a bright and gifted student who had tutored students at Kent State University to help them get their green cards (upon passing the high school equivalency test), was a far cry from the woman in front of me now.

My mother, Antoinette, for all her faults, had an amazing mind. Even during her crumbling and tumultuous marriages, she could still walk into any lawyer's office and convince them that she was a practicing paralegal (despite not graduating) due to how much law she had learned and studied on her own, teaching herself at the library, from a young age.

As I got older, I started to understand that some of my mother's unexplainable bitterness was born out of the dreams that she had thrown away just to survive and to give us a life. It was also her supreme knowledge that equipped her to teach Faith and me and homeschool us before she left John, and for a time, we were so far ahead of the other kids in our grade that when we would meet with our cousins in Warren, they would feel embarrassed that the random trivia that our uncle would throw at us, they couldn't really answer. But she never gave up on the dream that she would give us a life that was better than the one she had come from.

Then, my mother met John at college, and our lives changed forever.

CHAPTER 3:

New Family, New Life

Twin Lakes in Streetsboro was where that dream was manifested. John and Antoinette had married in a rushed court ceremony in Warren, and work at his new job, Pneumatic Scale, was flourishing. So, a new house in Twin Lakes, complete with two decks, a small pond in the backyard, and a fireplace, seemed like the natural next step. For seven years, it was truly the best times and moments of our lives when we finally had stability. We adopted two chocolate Labrador sisters, naming them Maxi, after John's last name, and Toni, my mom's nickname. We'd chase and play with them around the backyard and watched baby Melody play jubilantly in her baby walker, a gift that was given to us from our big stepsister, the rebellious Allie and biological daughter of John.

It really was the best and worst of times of my young life. Moments of perfection followed: going to the Twins Festival, even singing for a crowd of 10,000 together, going to see our first rodeo together as a family, the long car ride to Myrtle Beach for vacation, followed by summers at Six Flags and Cedar Point with year-round tickets were magical.

Playing Barbies was a way of life for the "bougie" homeschooled identical twin sisters Faith and Jordan. Playing Barbies in our decked-out playroom was our mission; we had just gotten some new outfits for them on a store run to Walmart while Mom got groceries more than twenty minutes away from the grassy countryside of Streetsboro.

My big stepsister, Allie's sixteen-year-old friends, Kiana and Tiana, were coming up to visit from Firestone.

Allie was trying to make peace with her biological dad, John, who was Faith and my stepfather officially now as of two years of marriage. Russian John and African American Antionette were truly trailblazers in the late '90s to early 2000s.

"Thank God that John isn't here," Allie said as soon as we walked in a grumbled tone, emphasizing that point, then went on. She was fiddling with a formula bottle for almost one-year-old Melody, who was fussy and relieved to see her nana's entrance, grasping for her.

"Ugh. Shut up, Mel! Thank God that he ain't here to tell me, in front of his own grandchild, that her father is a bastard negro. Or how good Faith and Jordan are. Ugh, anyway, y'all. How are y'all doin'? Tee, you get that pee stick result yet? Haha, girl, come on over here." Allie thought out loud to Key and Tee, helping my mom carry in shopping bags.

"Oh, Allie, don't start! Let these girls get in the house. Thanks, babies. Faith and Jordan will help you unload the groceries." Our mom's voice trailed off.

Even at ten, we could see our mother doing the spoil the friends, ignoring the daughter's treatment on Allie for once instead of us, so we shot her a look, then darted away upstairs quickly, laughing.

Allie was fussing with baby Melody to go to sleep, who was whining to join in our play despite having broken new toys in her toddler naïveté, so Faith and I used that moment to escape!

We rushed upstairs to get our favorite Barbies into their new cute outfits and moments later heard a hurried knock and excited squeal as Key and Tee ran in behind us as Allie and my mother Toni were starting to bicker.

Instead of hanging out with her, Ki and Ti would always want to hang out with us in our Barbie room, much to Allie's annoyance, we would later come to find. We even had a TV room off to the side, downstairs. Diagonal from our main living room and dining room, which had red mahogany, wood tables, and chairs, and the kitchen, complete with island granite countertops and stainless-steel refrigerator appliances.

The other side of the kitchen, behind the window bordering the end of the square counter center, was our homeschooling area.

Our homeschooling room had an alphabet bordering the walls, a large chalkboard, an easel in the corner for our painting and arts and crafts, a solar system poster, a calendar, Spanish verbs and basic numerology, a dry-erase board with markers, and photos of Harriet Tubman, Abraham Lincoln, and the current president at the time, Bill Clinton on the walls, among other things. Even some of our old friends we made in a semester at Fairlawn Elementary before our move to Streetsboro, friends Shayna and Chelsea, would visit and have sleepovers at our new home. We moved in at five years old and stayed until we were twelve years old before Antionette Brown and John Maksimovich split for good, per my mother's insistence not to raise us in fear, like she had been, come hell or highwater.

Back in Twin Lakes, down the steps from the homeschool kitchen area, to the right was the second TV room, which was at one point decked out in the inflatable blue and green chairs and couches that were popular in the early 2000s. Later, my mother opted for the more traditional suede couches while going full HGTV decorative on our bedroom designs. It was such a fun respite and get away. I just remember Kiana and Tiana coming over and visiting my sister and me, and even our Barbies, much to our delight. We literally had over 200 Barbies that we had collected over the years and kept with us during various moves, but we obviously lost some in the foster care drama. But in Twin Lakes, they were still in our Barbie world and next to our bedroom, in our playroom where NSYNC and Destiny's Child posters greeted you and stood like the billboards, and the big pink Barbie house was owned by the richest Barbie family in town, which came in rotation, based on which was our favorite barbie that week. Sometimes, it was our Brandy Norwood R&B singer's home, and her TV show family Moesha would ensue, or sometimes, it was the sorority-like house for our My Scene, Flava, and/or Bratz Dolls to vie over. Next, we had a bluish-gray medium-sized house for middle-class families and a couple of variations of those bordering the beige carpet in our Barbie World. A bluish airplane that was first used for trips but later became a trailer home for Faith's adorable new redheaded Barbie, Felecia, aka Fey.

In the Barbie's hair, you noticed the differences in the hair textures based on the races that the Barbie's were. Like my Hawaiian Barbie, which I named Natalia, how brushing her hair out would create volume that the redheaded, freckle face Barbie Felicia never had.

In a plot twist, I had her dating my Black Ken Doll Barbie Michael for a while in an act of defiance against her closed-minded, aircraft/trailer neighborhood family.

I remember Kiana and Tiana, at first, aghast at how seriously we were taking our game, us even chiding and chastising them over making their Barbies laugh at a bakery order at our Barbie Bakery Shop. They later got into the spirit of putting their personalities into their chosen archetype. I saw Kiana had begun splitting Barbie Fey's hair and delicately giving her cornrows, as her Beyoncé Barbie had unbraided her own micro braids into a crinkly mane but ready to re-braid her hair all over again. Ki and Ti even did Faith and me micro braids for various photoshoots my mother would take us to for cheer. Because Barbie Fey was becoming ethnic and melting into the melting pot of America, embracing other ethnicities, like so many girls she probably knew back in Akron.

We found a lot of great delight and would be giggling so hard that my mom would even join in sometimes. She always wanted to pull out the boom box and Barbie stage, and we would play Showtime at the Apollo. We'd grab one of our mom's carefully crafted small ceramic Pier One bowls and use it as the "good luck" rock the contestants would rub on the show, and Momma Toni would grab the Barbie microphones, plug in the stage so the lights illuminated the whole room, disco ball kaleidoscopes would fill the room and we would put in Destiny Child's "The Writing's on the Wall" CD, and even some Selena CDs that mom got us after watching the Jennifer Lopez *Selena* film. It was great because sometimes our stepdad would even join in, grateful for the lighthearted respite of his serious engineering job at Pneumatic Scale. And he would either be the judge or hilariously off-tune singer, grabbing the white male surfer like twin boy doll, Blaine, and Shane Barbies, as his self, and we would just be cracking up dying of laughter, as we called it, on the floor for hours, letting out chuckles and letting loose until our stomach's hurt. Kiana and Tiana and my cousin Jalisa would always join in, and even baby Melody and John. Allie would sit sullenly on the couch, rolling her eyes, but she couldn't ruin our joyous moment.

Then my mom would make some of her delicious meals; her specialty was sauerkraut and kielbasa, she would make that on New Year's, or she would make the spicy spaghetti and meatballs that were such an intricate made sauce. It was a recipe that she kept with her, but anyway, she was an amazing cook. Beyond that, she would also make fried green tomato sandwiches; she loved tomatoes, so she would make tomato soup and grilled cheeses for snacks.

CHAPTER 4:

Beginning of the Storm

After we had moved from Warren to Akron with John and Allie as a family, and then eventually Twin Lakes, we were getting adjusted to our new life. My mom still wanted us to keep our faith in Christ, and she knew that that wasn't possible in Streetsboro due to the harsh prejudices in the area.

Even so, Faith and I started going to school for second and third grade, as we were already enrolled in Pee-Wee Cheerleading through the school. However, we, unfortunately, started to experience a lot of racism and microaggressions from the kids at school. Faith and I were the only black students in the whole school besides this one Middle Eastern boy in a different grade.

Even before the new school year began, as Faith and I got our new bikes and were exploring Twin Lakes riding our bikes around, we were confronted by two blonde boys and a brunette boy that were circling around us like little sharks and smirking and even throwing out hurls like, "Uhh look, two blackies! You're so dark. Eew, look at your legs! And your dark knees!" they taunted as they raced away laughing.

Faith and I shouted back, "Leave us alone, racist freaks! We don't even know you, like what's your problem!" and we knew that this was setting the tone for how school was going to be. Later, we would finally be home-schooled by our brilliant mother, Antionette, but this is the part where we gave them a chance.

One day, coming home from school on the school bus, I had just finished up my second day of second grade, and I saw some kids a few seats behind me laughing and hollering.

Papers were being crunched up and thrown at a boy diagonal from me, they were making fun of him because his parents worked at McDonald's.

"Ha-ha — we know he didn't get anything for Christmas! Your mom works at McDonald's. You probably got socks!" A boy shouted into the crowd of uproarious laughter. I saw the boy try to slide down in his seat more and I tried to shoot him a passing encouraging glance.

However, the following week, for picture day, it would be my turn.

"Mommy, I'm really nervous. I don't want to go. Those kids are so cruel… he can't help where his parents work," I said woefully as my mom pinned a pendant on my paisley shawl.

She tried to get my courage up and said, "Go grab my purse. I'll let you get a couple of brushes of lipstick. Just a little now, miss thing!"

At seven, this was a rare treat. I beamed at the pale green silky dress my mom bought me.

I was so excited when my outfit was complete. Faith had opted for her favorite pastel pink, and we were off to school.

School went well; a couple of girls even silently giggled and told us, "Hey, cute dresses, twins," in passing.

We parted ways and went to our separate classes.

The day seemed to be going well until I got to art class. Here, people had assigned seats, and as soon as I entered the room, all heads turned to me, and the room filled with heavy tension.

The teacher stammered, then said, "Come in and sit, Jordan. Don't feel shy. Class, this is Jordan, our new student. Make some room for her, everyone, scoot down."

"Today, we're learning about Picasso and the contrast of colors. Brights and darks," the teacher said, and I sat down at the end edge of the table because there wasn't enough room for me next to a very sullen-looking, pale-faced boy with dark hair. The teacher next instructed, "Okay, students, grab the white paints and black paints to start filling in the squares to show me that you understand comparing and contrasting."

As we began to paint, I realized I had no paint near me, so I asked one of the students, who was busy at work, and then I asked the boy next to me, "Can you please pass me the black paint?" because I knew I could just tell in his expression that he was already uncomfortable with my sitting next to him and was sort of testing him to see how far these kids would go.

He ignored me for about ten minutes, and then as the bell was starting to ring, he muttered, "Why don't you just wipe your hand on the page," and then got up, and everyone hurried out, and I just sat there.

Finally, the time for picture day came, and I couldn't really muster up a genuine smile, but I still have my picture day photo of that, and it's beautiful. I'll add photos I managed to salvage at the end. I had a small little smile and got a few compliments from some of the girls in my class on my dress.

Finally, I caught up with Faith as we were lining up for the bus.

"How was your picture? Mine turned out really cute," I said to my sister.

To which she replied, "It's okay, I guess. The girls in line were pushing me and not letting me sit down. I hate this school for real."

As we were filling in line for the bus to go home, other kids were shuffling the crowd, and I briefly lost touch with my sister. As I was climbing onto the bus, there was a big mud puddle next to it that everybody was trying to avoid.

I cleverly hopped over a couple and then kind of chuckled in the laughter at being able to preserve my dress when an older boy that was trying to get to his mother's car shoved past me and cruelly sneered,

"Ha-ha little niglet over here, one o'clock" and pushed me into the mud puddle, ruining my beautiful dress.

That night, I was relaying the story to my mother tearfully and said, "Why can't God just make us white? I mean, if we're not supposed to be black, or if people hate us for being black. Daddy is Russian, and he loves you, so why is everyone else like this? I hate this! If I was white, my life would be way easier."

My mom sat me down and told me, "I know it's hard. Come here, baby. But you should never be ashamed of your brown skin. Look at how many powerful people in history have skin just like yours. Never say that you wish you were white, baby. You know how I always tell you, 'This is a don't care world,' honey? Remember when we were learning about slavery and Harriet Tubman, and later about the Cotton Club era and the brown paper bag rule that they had for those girls? Well, that's how our country was built, and unfortunately, it really wasn't all that long ago that your grandma Idella was a little girl and was forced to sit in the back of the bus growing up just for being a black girl."

"Remember babies," she said as Faith joined our huddle on the couch, "It's not those kids' fault. It's their parent's fault, their ignorant, jerky parents — excuse my French — because their parents were raised incorrectly and kept that vicious, hateful cycle going on. Hate isn't natural. It's something that is taught and ingrained in them and from a young age too. The way that memory Bible verses are ingrained into you, so I think I'm going to look into our church, Ebeneezer Baptist, our old church from Warren, so that you can start being around some more diversity, some more kids that look like you."

In retrospect, I realize that this was the early 1990s, and it was still very taboo for people to see interracial couples in general, especially in the lily-white area like Twin Lakes, and then even more so because a black woman was with a white man and not a black man being with a white woman.

CHAPTER 5:

Culture Clashing Upbringing

So Ebeneezer Baptist Church in Warren became our connection to rekindling our family bond with relatives that lived there, and Faith and I eagerly anticipated these trips to go and visit because we knew we would get to play and let loose with our cousins after that. We'd still be in our church stockings and dresses, and when we were coming to Aunt Ella's cloudy, smoky kitchen, we would immediately grab Layla and Tori's hand, exclaiming, "We need play clothes!" and then rush to change into some of their shorts and tee-shirts, running outside in the yard to meet little JJ and other neighborhood kids.

My cousin JayJay would toss the football toward me, and we'd play flag football. It was all very new to me because I was more so just used to cheerleading and playing with my puppies at home and in the pond in the backyard at Twin Lakes, stealing frogs and trying to keep them as pets, on a dare for my stepdad.

Sometimes, my other aunt Sharon's kids would be there, and then it would be a full house and we would just be whizzing by going from different house to house of our friends.

We'd giggle and sneak and go into friend's freezers to grab popsicles then hop on the back end of our cousin's bike, ready to be whizzed away to the next spot.

One time, Faith had on her pink Barbie skirt, pale pink lace shirt, and heels from church, and she was trying to hop right in step with Layla, who wanted to race with Faith.

Instead of changing, she decided to hop on the back of her bike, but Faith still had her heels on, and I just remember her tumbling down and looking like a little Tinker Bell just like with her hair and everything going around and like a little pink furball.

We all gasped briefly, but she got right back up and was like, "Come on, guys, let's go. Come on, yo."

So, in the flurry of our childhood fun, we would then come back home to settle down and get ready for school the next day and catch up and see what Jalisa and others were doing in school, etc.

My mom would cheerfully brag about Faith and me learning Spanish and our cheerleading, but she never really got into our school setting because she was still in the works to pull us out of the racist school we were in and start her own schooling with the Board of Education. She was creating her own curriculums in homeschooling us, which she began that same year.

My aunt Ella exclaimed, "Spanish? Who do they think they are, some rich, white kids? Why do they need to know that?"

My mom always would defend education vehemently, saying, "When Ebert had that upstart car rental business, who did the bookkeeping and budgeting when they were twelve? It wasn't you, so thank you."

Aunt Ella would scoff under her breath and usher in or call Ebert, my mother's stepfather, to come visit.

Ebert always came and gloated about Jalisa and JayJay's straight As.

"Yeah, well, y'all being homeschooled, you don't have a report card to show." Ebert would say to Faith and me.

My mom would retort, "They just performed a stadium field show with their cheerleading squad in Kent; they'll be just fine."

Our cousins, noticing the tone shift, would snicker in sudden agreement, "Yeah, y'all weird, always askin' if somebody a Christian, haha," and scurry off.

I'd hear my mom mutter under her breath, "Yeah, straight As in that ghetto rundown school. It's not really much to write home about."

The family dynamic of my mother being treated differently after the air of excitement from childhood play wore off was noticeable for all of us.

So, we would literally go from playing jubilantly to being in the crossfire of years-long tensions of my mother being abused, but it never really been acknowledged. Rather, hidden under the surface behind passive aggression.

Ebert would burst in the door, and then the tone with shift completely, and I realized that even if you have a bond with family, if it's not built on authenticity and mutual respect, then it can't really truly flourish into real love.

Even so, without the presence of Ebert, I still would have some great memories with my cousins when old family drama wasn't involved and forced us to take a side.

Thanksgiving was always the time that our family from Warren would try to reconnect, and at Twin Lakes, it became a lavish event. My aunts and cousins and John's Russian relatives from Kent all came pouring into our house. For these more intricate dinners, Mom would make steak kebabs, turkey, of course, pineapple-seasoned ham, and fried chicken. All the meats were so ornately done you could taste that all the spices were made from scratch. The meat would absorb a lot of the flavor as it marinated in the spices, and her stuffing was made with breadcrumbs from scratch. Also, for her apple cinnamon cheesecake or strawberry original flavor, she always made the crumb cake from scratch, then used fresh strawberries, flour, and cream cheese for the cake.

Family from Warren, Uncle Jay, Jalisa, little JayJay, and my other cousins came pouring in, Aunt Ella's collard greens and mac and cheese in tow to compete with my mother's. Aunt Ella's mac and cheese turned out to be dryer in comparison to my mother's milkier version, and I remember Uncle JJ laughingly telling her to take notes, as my mother emphasized to use almond milk instead of diluting it with water, as she looked away rolling her eyes.

Allie's elderly Russian aunt, Darlene, came waddling in, bringing her own stuffing and green bean casserole. Faith and my cousin played, throwing over our deck into the snow and trying to feed it to our chocolate labs, chasing us.

For all the family issues, during these sweet moments, my uncle Jay still always made a point of saying, "Hey beautiful!" to Faith and me in his jolly and cheerful way whenever he did get to see us after a long time of not seeing each other. I always remembered and cherished that side of him when things were positive and not always so negative.

These memories are so precious, and I'm glad that even on hard days, you can always read a page of your memories in photos and step right back into that happy place. That grateful place. Because so many others don't have that blessing.

Yet these beautiful memories and moments we made were always coupled with the chaos that was brewing and bubbling just under the surface.

On the car ride back from the rodeo, my dad got mad at something my mom had said during the car ride and started screaming, yelling belligerently, and acting like he was going to run us all off the road and saying that he would take us all down with them if it came to it just a reminder to young me how fragile our life was becoming.

Back home in Streetsboro, it was two weeks before Christmas. Stepdad John is sitting next to Faith on our beige sofa while Faith flips Boy Meets World on Disney channel, getting taught the trinkets of the remote to go with our fancy new flat screen TV, very 2000s style that took up a good chunk of the corner living room floor. I laid on the fireplace cobblestone hearth with the Brandy "Moesha" Norwood Barbie doll in tow with the Mary Kate and Ashley tweenager Barbies along with the Beyoncé and Kelly Barbies, making them dance and swing their micro braids and bobs in the air. Eventually, Faith got bored with the TV and joined me.

"What if our house burns down?" Faith made her Ashley Olsen Barbie say in a flurry, where my Brandy Barbie retorted, "Are you kidding me? If our stuff caught fire, we'd just put it out with the snow, duh!" Faith and I stared at each other for a moment, then busted out in laughter at the idea of us throwing snowball clumps at a raging fire.

Ironically enough, that comment made in innocent jest became all too real one night when we had all come back home from viewing neighboring houses ornate in Christmas decorations, glittering white lights outlined and rimmed storybook-looking houses, and sparkling white snow blanketed the ground.

Our own walkway was always lined with candy canes every year, a tradition my mom lovingly started back in Warren on Dunstan Drive to solidify our fresh start from Chicago and the new house being made into a home. Only that a billowing dark smoke came rushing out of the right-hand side of our roof, and white smoke filled the air as Faith and I were rushed to our van as John fought the indoor sprinklers to try and extinguish the fire.

A week before Christmas, our home was now not only lit up with our white Christmas lights, but the frantic red and blue lights of the fire truck and police cruiser beaming over the thick black smoke. Our mom had run in after buckling us in to hurriedly grab night clothes, a couple of dolls, and quick items for herself before John came rushing back, informing us that his insurance would be covering our damages and a hotel stay.

The catch, he said, was that it was at a company upstart hotel called Microtel, and it lived up to its name.

On our hurried ride to the accommodation hotel, the EMT told us, "Your fireplace, ma'am. Not the main one in the living room but the second chimney, over on the right end of the house. The chimney in the family den was very old and there was a ton of dirt and fiber, and the wall was completely lined with that had gone up in flames. We found some family photos and videos and a couple of present boxes that were totally cindered, ma'am." He briefly paused as my mother let out a shocked gasp, and he attempted to put her at ease. "But don't worry, Mrs. Finley, we managed to extinguish all the fiber that was stuck in the chimney lining. However, the boys are still workin' on that side part. We're afraid… we're afraid that the flames, we got to 'em too late, and they took off a good portion of your roof before it was fully stopped."

I just remember our pretty white Christmas lights and candy cane-lined walkway and then the flames above it around the chimney.

Anyway, in Microtel, it was extremely small and microscopic, hence the name. The beds were full-sized, but the microwave, the kitchen, cabinets, and space were suffocatingly small for us four. During that month or so, while our house was repaired, John eventually got us upgraded to the extended-stay hotel.

My mom and dad were arguing even more in the nights now, and in that confined space, the fracture of their marital bond became glaringly clear.

Yet even so, our mother, formidable as ever in the pursuit of pouring knowledge into us girls, read up on the new Anne Frank miniseries movie adaptation airing in 2000. She had us watch the miniseries, even if she had just had to end a screaming match mid-sentence. She wanted Faith and I to watch the book we had finished reading in our homeschooling, *The Diary of a Young Girl*. The harrowing realism of the dehumanization of the Jewish people was so poignant at times, with the race issue hitting closer to home to the Russian John, causing him to become sullen and withdrawn after particularly bitter depictions of the concentration camp life forced upon them. My mother's expert way of thinking made its impact by the time we returned home for a belated Christmas celebration to open our presents, and a newer, gentler side to my stepdad emerged for a time. He relented and said he wouldn't fight Mommy on taking Faith and me back to Warren to our old church home, Ebeneezer Baptist, where we had frequented occasionally but really began to miss it even though things were hard at school, and it just became a monumental statement piece for my life.

Next came the Ebeneezer Baptist choir poem contest. The choice of my mother to start going back to church was causing a bigger rift between John and my mom. I saw him peering in on our prayer times at night, but mostly drinking more and distancing himself from us after his long work shifts. Even still, my mother persisted and kept Faith and me disciplined with weekly memory Bible verses to turn into her after our schoolwork.

Before the big day to recite our poem aloud, our mom had us write several rough draft soliloquy poems on how we felt God had empowered us and black women through history, referencing a Bible character, a historical figure (I picked Harriet Tubman and Esther, Faith picked Rosa Parks and Mary) and a Bible verse reference in the poem contest at church.

As twins, our poem rendition received an uproarious reception and applause from our church members and a cheek-to-cheek photo opportunity with our beloved T. D. Jakes-esque-like pastor, Pastor Walker, filling us with theological verve and insight for our futures.

That summer came our big parade cheer for the Raiders, with our cheer squad performing for a mile-long celebration. NSYNC's "Bringin' the Noise" permeated our cheer field and our playroom as we bounced on our neon blow-up couches and rehearsed our performances religiously.

When it came time for photos, however, the stage mom in our normally bubbly mother would emerge, and instead of directions came terse shouts of, "Move over and pose right, idiot! I'm paying way too much money for these photographs for your bratty little self to mess it up!" Followed by a twisted pinch into my shoulder and the threat of a "whoopin'" (as we called it) if I didn't comply.

This swift change in my mother's demeanor to darkness would only become more prevalent as times changed.

I realized that the photo was taken moments before my mom's brief interruption and was captured by the photographer before I had a chance to correct my reactive facial expression. My mother was always the hardest on me, even though we were twins, and the photo showed a beaming Faith with a subdued me.

I wish I could've faked it for that photo, but in retrospect to where my life turned, it seems fitting that it remains a part of my story.

During the school year, our homeschool trips were our main way to get outside and keep up with and eventually surpass the kids at public school.

On one trip, Faith and I were bakers for a day at the Pie Factory at Quaker Square, bringing home a few historical tips but, most importantly, some delicious homemade apple and cherry pies.

After that, we visited the Cosi Museum in Columbus, Ohio.

The memory of a ten-year-old me riding a unicycle attached to a wire string suspended in midair to learn about gravity. I remember peering out of my mother's red Audi, looking up at the skyscrapers and cleaning my neck, and still not even being able to see the top of it, and just being in awe that my mom, through her rheumatism and physical pain, working through a strained marriage, still managed all that and to teach us so much.

She even learned how to drive a stick shift in the new red Audi John had recently bought her. She would stall out, putting the gear up, down, sideways, before yelling out in exasperation in some pretty hilarious moments on steep hills. Watching her push through, she pushed herself past her own limits time and time again while she raised us and taught me how to do the same through her actions, which will always be louder than her words.

Next, we were onto an arts and culture lesson, a slavery reenactment tour in Hudson with our homeschooled group. We never saw them except for field trips.

On the trail we walked along with our tour we actually retraced the very same footsteps of runaway slaves.

We were guided to hide in a barn while we waited for our abolitionist relief to drive the soldiers away. For about ten minutes, we stood there in eerie and cold silence and listened for the sound of our helpers, arriving in horse and buggy, with our main guide lying underneath the hay.

A loud bang shook the frail barn walls.

"You got fugitive slaves out here, don't ya, boy!" a bellowing man's voice shouted out. The slave catchers were here. They banged on the doors, "Any fugitive negro we find will be liable to be shot or hung by the neck until he is dead!"

Our tour group seemed as if it had swallowed itself; each bang rang through us. I noticed the people jolted at his words but never let the tension be heard.

All we could see was the glare of moonlight creeping in from the very top of the stable as the dust from every rap to the door settled into the air.

I learned how everyone would naturally react in this way if they were faced with the same circumstances and how realistic it was.

The actors even recited the new law that had passed in the time period we were portraying, 1865, the Fugitive Slave Act, which had been passed during the onslaught of Nat Turner's infamously bloody slave revolt and, subsequently, the Civil War.

At the beginning of the tour, we sat outside by the tiki torchlight at dusk going into the evening and watched the performers on stage interlude on who we were portraying and what time period we were in. Ohio was emphasized as a free state.

Following the reenactors from the barn, we walked along a dark path with billowy trees shading our steps and along the riverside to use the water to mask or scent because the bloodhounds were always immediately put on any slave who dared to dream as a human being.

Even though that experience was powerful, I truly believe spiritual warfare was going on after my mom decided to take us back to Ebeneezer Baptist Church because my stepdad was becoming more staunchest against the idea. John decided that he didn't want us to be raised believing in anything, but my mom persisted. But his screaming rants and raves and random outbursts that were heard through the walls would always be prevalent.

Anyways, a few months after the housefire, another real-life shock would be headed our way.

CHAPTER 6:

Twin's Festival Memory — Singing for 10,000

Not before the Twin's festival, though, where Faith and I had choir practice for weeks on end, getting our notes just right, at Ebeneezer Baptist church. The Twin's festival turned out to be a huge success and extravaganza. There were mini-rollercoaster rides, face painting booths, twin boy and girl sets in matching outfits, taking photos, cherry funnel cakes, and more.

I remember that at the last minute, our mom managed to convince Allie to bring baby Melody and join us, as she and John had been attempting to reconcile. Baby Melody enjoyed the carousel as we looked on lovingly at her jubilant wave at us. My mom found every opportunity to pose us with pairs of twins. We looked up in awe. It was a blindingly hot and bright summer day in Twinsburg. I know I still have a few photos from that day of Faith and me; it's hard to keep up with photos with so many moves. I'll add a couple I do have. There was so much music and excitement going on and pressure from our mom to perform. Most people seemed to be having fun simply seeing and meeting all of the twins!

In between photos, more stressed-out warnings behind the scenes from our mom, occasionally hissing orders into Faith's ear and mine, I saw her pinching Faith one time. Anyway, this caused some of these photos to warrant grimacing smiles from both Faith and me, yet we still managed to capture some great moments between us and other sets of twins and even some triplets.

We were sitting playing patty cake with baby Melody and joking around over corn dogs when Mommy came rushing over to us from a white tent with event coordinators. She surprised Faith and me with the news at lunch.

"Guess what, babies! I just got those ladies to look at you and told them of what great singers you are, that you just won a poem contest and performed the Twinsburg parade, and they want you to hear you sing 'Yes, Jesus Loves Me!' Come on, girls, we have to get over there!"

In a minute, Momma Toni had us two, along with Melody's stroller, being pushed by a panting Allie, trying to keep up with us between the swarms of people. Our mom made a swift beeline toward a growing and roaring crowd.

"But Mommy," Faith stammered, trying to get out of it, "I — I can't do it; there's too many people!"

"You sang for the entire church at Ebeneezer! And you've been singing that song since you were babies; I don't want to hear it! Now, wipe your face and put some more lip gloss on; you're about to be on!" she roared to Faith while hurriedly writing something on her notepad that she was about to rip out and hand the waving and gesturing DJ.

"Come on, sweeties, you're up next." The gentleman motioned for Faith and me to walk backstage and wait as the current act went on.

"And now here with us are identical twin sisters and choir singers at their church, Ebenezeer, Jordan and Faith Finley," the announcer carefully announced, reading a piece of paper my mother had slipped him.

The microphone whistled and crackled in my quivering hand. I counted and looked to Faith, she knew to start singing on five. One. Two. Three. Four.

Faith stammered, "Yeah. Yes. Je-he-sus. Loves... me."

And I rushed in, annoyed, but quickly covered it up to fill in where she was offbeat, "Yes, Jesus… loves me-ee."

In unison, "Yes. Je-he-sus. Loves… me."

"Yes, Jesus… loves me-ee."

"Yes, Jesus… loves me!"

"For the *Bibol*. Tells. Me-ee. So."

"Lit-tle ones to Him belong. We are weak, but He is strong."

"Yes. Jesus loves me. For the *Bibull*. Tells. Me-e. So."

A moment of pause. The audience wasn't expecting a gospel. We gasped and heard a cry of "Woohoo! Go, girls!" to uproarious applause. It was an unforgettable moment that I can truly say I'm grateful for.

The good moment would always be followed by a sudden shock, and the shock came with a beehive infestation that was building and about to hit very close to home for me. Going into spring that following year, I heard rustling over my bed in the walls.

An enormous beehive was growing over my bed inside the walls. My wall had gone from white to some yellow stain, and it kept growing.

I showed my mom, and she called the exterminator. The exterminator guys came with the beehive with astronaut-looking uniforms and gas face masks and went into the room. They came out about forty-five minutes later and told us that the whole room had swarmed with bees.

He held what looked to be a twenty-pound honeycomb and chuckled somewhat nervously, saying, "*Whew!* You're lucky, kid. If you would have waited another week, this whole thing would have dropped on your head. Your ceiling wall was so thin we could actually poke a pencil and push it through, and then that's when all hell broke loose."

My mother gasped, "Are you saying it could have killed her if it fell through?"

The exterminator looked at me and sized the honeycomb up next to me. "With her tiny frame and size… hate to say it, but yeah. It would have definitely killed her. Her sister's bed was closer to the door, and she could've escaped. But not her with the whole hive on her face. *Whew*. Lucky kid!"

CHAPTER 7:

Storm Continues

While the stability of our family seemed to be ebbing and flowing, going up and down like a precarious hill, things with Allie and John would finally come to a head once and for all.

Allie and Darius had moved into the spacious finished basement and were attempting to make it work as one big family. Darius was baby Melody's transient father, who was only two years out of the penitentiary for selling drugs. From his time in the penitentiary, he had somehow contracted and spread herpes, a sexually transmitted disease, to Allie while she was pregnant with Melody.

Yet Darius had managed to secure a factory job that hired felons that my mom had found him, but he had just been fired from it, and John was furious.

"What about the time out in Warren, when he had my kid bent over bawling on the bed, and Toni had you with the tweezers picking out the red crabs in her pubic hair that worthless bum gave her!"

"But John, it's still the middle of winter, the middle of the night! Where are two kids going to go with a baby in the middle of the snow?" Mom cried.

"I don't give a heck. You, outside!" John yelled in-distinctively and rattled the house, yanking Darius out into the cold.

I rushed Faith up the stairs to find Allie in the guest room that we had turned from John's office into Allie's nursery while they set up their apartment in the basement.

"Allie, wait! Stop packing! You don't have to leave! Besides, where are you gonna go?" I pleaded, horrified to think of little Melody, who was still peacefully sleeping in her bassinet, watching the *Prince of Egypt* movie with Faith and me in the den.

"Yeah, Allie. Even if he leaves, you can stay till things cool down!" Faith chimed in, touching one of Melody's crochet socks.

Allie grabbed it from her hand, "Stop. It's useless, kid. Look, you don't know him, not like I do. You never iced your mother's lip after one of his drunken episodes, so I don't wanna hear a little kid that doesn't know jack about the world tell me anything! Got it? Now, hand me that rag. Don't worry, okay? Darius has people we can stay with, so stop acting so dramatic." She finished with a fleshy scoff and zipped up Melody's diaper bag. I was deeply offended by her harsh tone but knew as a child that there wasn't anything me or Faith could do to stop her from leaving.

Even still, we pleaded and begged and followed her to the family room, where Melody was slowly waking up in a sleepy whine.

I picked her up. "Shh, Mel. It's okay, go back to sleep, little baby."

She started to soothe, but Allie ripped her out of my arms and strapped her in her car seat.

"You're not her mom, Jordan! Back off!" she roared, and with a flip of her coat, she flung the door open into the flurrying snow.

We could make out Mommy in between Darius and John, who had his hands around Darius' throat, begging him to let him go.

"Please, John! You see, the cops are on their way! Stop this madness and just let them go. She said she's going to call me as soon as she gets where she's going!"

John growled and shoved Darius harder into his van, screaming, "I let you come into my home, and this is what you do? Knock my daughter up, then get fired from the one job my wife slaved for you to get? You take my granddaughter into some crack house, and I'll kill you! Do. You. Hear me?"

We heard Darius' breath grunt and saw the cop car lights zero in on our house again.

A few neighbors' lights peered on.

Eventually, we saw the cop intervene. Mommy explained that they were living with us. Allie hurriedly threw Melody's car seat in the back of this idling van; she screamed that John was a racist prick and that she'd die before she set foot back in this house. Finally, the cop affirmed that Darius was leaving and told John to make sure he filed a police report.

Things were sullen and hollow with baby Melody's playful innocence gone and the worry of where she and Allie were.

We kept busy with our learning. I went on from PeeWee to JV Junior Varsity cheerleading for tweens in Streetsboro, and despite my parents' lackadaisical approach to remaining consistent, I even convinced them to take me to cheer at a couple of games.

I remember John took me to practice because Faith had given up on cheerleading and was more focused on her flute lessons, writing short stories, and reading. She was more-so hooked on the *Babysitter's Club* books and R. L Stine's *Fear Street* collection and with growing out her natural nails with our mom.

They bonded over nail polish and were very obsessed with their nails being in different lacquers. They would even fight over Sally Hansen's topcoat nail polish. I stuck with cheerleading practice and rehearsing my routines, begging my mom to take me to practices so I wouldn't fall behind. My mom was more caught up with keeping tabs on John's infidelity and now Allie and Melody's homelessness than with our extracurriculars.

I started pleading with my mom to bring my friends from the squad over and have us stretch together in my playroom and catch up on NSYNC and Backstreet Boys. Brandy and Destiny's Child were new to them. Even though our squad was multiracial, in the suburbs during the mid-1990s, cultural awareness was still a far cry from what it is today.

There was an underlying racial tension within our group. We even went to see the *Bring It On* movie about racial tensions in high school together when it premiered as a squad, and it helped us bond.

But anyway, the cheerleading practice challenge we were working on was how to do a toe touch stunt and a herkie jump and how to perform them seamlessly back-to-back.

I kept practicing it for weeks, and one time, I stayed up later at night and woke John up one time. I remember even him laughing yet impressed with my commitment, jokingly saying, "I'm gonna throw out you and that NSYNC tape into oncoming traffic; that'll be bringing the dang on the noise!" before he grabbed me up in tickles and put me to bed.

My stepdad John decided to take me to the field game and said, "This will be all by yourself now, Jordy. You earned it." I remember it felt like an out-of-body experience to do anything without my twin sister by my side. But he whispered encouragingly, "You can do this!" And I ran to catch up with warmups.

Finally, the big moment came; our music came on, and we were center stage on the field, doing our routine in perfect unison. I noticed John's eyes staring, and it pushed me to land my toe touch higher than I had before, and as we were leaving, the girls were giving me high-fives.

As we were heading to the car, he was encouraging and told me, "You had it all! Wow. You did those touches just like all the other girls. I'm proud of you." Tears came to my eyes as I thought to myself, though things may be uncertain, in these good moments, I was truly blessed for these experiences.

John and his persistence are what edged his way slowly then quickly into our lives and forever changed the course of my life. From Warren to Youngstown, with promises "to give my mom and us the life we deserved," we moved. The beginning of countless moves began for me. From Alden Elementary in Warren to Fairlawn Elementary in Akron began our vicious cycle of one day a happy home to a hairs trigger event resulting in a violent argument that could send either my mom or dad into a hysteria, screaming at each other, then throwing clothes into garbage bags or throwing glass objects around, and Allie, Faith, and I being caught in the middle.

As I adjusted to my new normal at Secure Treatment Center in Berea, all these memories came flooding back to me. Even though I was only seventeen at the time, I felt like I had lived several different lives over the span of their ten-year marriage, probably because of all the constant moving.

When I was eleven, their marriage came ahead for the last time. At this point of their breaking up and getting back together, in the midst of one of their breakups. John had sold our home in Twin Lakes after a particularly dramatic fight had caused Allie to flee with Melody away from the chaos in the middle of the night again, after a brief reconciliation, and my mom had decided to haul Faith and me back to Warren to "start over for good," she said. John's drinking, his cheating, and the alleged abuse that I never witnessed but would always hear through the walls.

However, John wasn't going to take that lying down, and he didn't accept one of the last breakups they had had, so he decided to show up in our townhome in Cuyahoga Falls Hunter's Lake with a gun in his pants to great Faith and me as we got off the bus.

Even though he was paying all the bills there and taking care of us, if his temper got out of control, my mom would pack up his things or throw them out the window or the door and make him go live in a hotel. Then randomly, weeks later, I would wake up and see his work boots and know that our family was back on for the moment.

CHAPTER 8 :

The Scary Marriage —
Suburbs to Divorce then
Foster Care

"Your mom says she's leaving and taking you with her. But it's not all up to her. She can't — she can't just take my family away from me," he said, slowly gesturing to his pistol, and the glistening in his eyes was emblazoned, staring directly at us.

The sweet dad that I knew who would sing with Faith and me and say we were in a rock band called "JJF" as we played hooky from school sometimes to get ice cream at McDonald's was no longer there.

Faith and I stood there frozen and stunned, our backpacks still on. Faith started having a nosebleed right there on the floor, and John rushed to get a napkin.

As soon as he turned his back, I told Faith to run upstairs and call Mommy at work. "I don't care if she doesn't answer, just keep calling her and tell her Daddy's here."

She rushed upstairs without a word.

Daddy came back. "What's wrong with Faithy? Did I scare you? Oh, I didn't mean that," he said and picked me up like he used to when I was sick or fell asleep in the car. "Did you miss me?" He winked, and at first, I was tempted to let my guard down and fall right back in as the tomboy/daddy's girl I had been going fishing at the lake... but then I felt his gun on his hip and got back down.

"Yes, Daddy. I mean, of course, I missed you… but I've missed you for a long time. I missed you when I was seven, too. Remember when you came back, and I was so happy to see you?"

"Yes." He laughed a little, sitting next to me on the couch. "You were almost buried in the snow trying to get me, and I scooped you up and held you close just like now."

"No, Daddy, it's not just like now. Mommy doesn't know you're here, and Faith's worried and — "

"Where is Faith? She didn't come back down. Faith, get down here right now!" His familiar authoritarian voice was back. Faith came downstairs in a rush, darting towards the downstairs bathroom.

"Jordan, I need you in the bathroom." She closed the door in a rush; it was holding our emergency flip phone. "Mommy's phone keeps going straight to voicemail; she won't answer."

"Jordan," I heard him start.

"I got to go in there and keep him calm; keep trying to call Mommy," I whispered and hid the phone in her jeans pocket.

"Come in here and sit down with me. What's all this whispering I hear?" he said, opening the door. Faith glided out just out of his reach, and I walked with him back to the couch. Faith sat on the armrest, and I sat in between them to try and make Faith more comfortable, but he picked me up so that he was in the middle. "How was school? Getting good grades? Any boyfriends… ?" he quipped, elbowing me. We knew that something was wrong with him; he usually didn't act this desperate, this emotional, and his eyes had that crazy look in them like when he was about to do something impulsive.

"You know Mommy says we're too young for boyfriends," Faith said quietly.

"Hah. Is that right? Your mother says a lot of things, you know. Like how she wants to leave me, but then calls crying, saying she needs money… I can't keep up with her."

"Why do you have a gun?" Faith muttered solemnly.

"You know why," he said, getting creepily friendly again. "It's for protection." Then, he pulled out a newspaper. "You know, I read a really interesting story in here, an article right before the bus dropped you two off. It was about a man, a homeless man, that a woman started taking care of. She felt sorry for him because he was sick. She starts making him dinner, taking care of him."

"Daddy, you're being creepy," Faith said, slowly trying to edge away.

"Just listen to the story," he barked and made Faith sit back down. "So, the lady goes to sleep one night and tells him to leave, but when she wakes up, he's on top of her. He's on the inside of her having sex," he says the last word slowly, adding emphasis.

Faith leaps up and goes to the computer, but John, growing annoyed, blocks her and says, "Your mother is the cause of all this, you know? All this pain and everything. The fact that you don't even have a normal childhood. I wanted to give you stability. But your mother and this fake fibromyalgia stuff." We were taken aback by his profane mood but always knew that our Mommy's fibromyalgia was a real issue that she battled, and we would be there for her through it even if he chose not to.

Faith runs over to me and hugs me, saying, "Just get away from us; why are you even here? You know you don't really care about us anyway."

He lurches over to her, saying, "Don't use that kind of language with me."

I stand in the middle with my hands up, saying, "Whoa, whoa, wait a minute. Just please calm down. Mommy will be here soon."

"You bet your little jerk she'll be here. Wait for her. And she's not taking you two anywhere."

Just then, the door flings open. In Mommy walks, keys rattling, looking down at the blood droplets on the floor from Faith's nosebleed.

"What's happened? I left my phone in the car, and I saw I have like twenty missed calls, and now there's blood on the floor? John, what have you done to my babies?" she starts slowly then her voice grows louder.

"I haven't done anything." He scoffs, then shoves Faith towards her, then he grabs my shoulder and shows his gun, pointing to my side. "You're done taking my family from me, Toni. Jordan said she wants to move with me and get away from your crazy self," he roared.

"No, I didn't. I never said that. Mommy, please!" I cried.

"Run!" Mommy screams, tossing Faith the keys to her red Audi, "Start it up just like I showed you. Jordan, go help her!"

In an instant, Mommy shoves herself right in Daddy's face, and we dart for the car. I hear them screaming and clamoring and eventually hear the jingle of her keys and know she's not too far behind us.

As Mommy lurches into the driver's seat, Faith falls over to the passenger, and Mommy starts pulling out while her door's still open.

We hear Daddy bellowing, "I can't believe you're doing this again. I said stop, God!" as he dashes in his blue Camaro and peels out after us.

"We have to lose him. Put on your seatbelts, babies!" Mommy cries.

Eventually, we circled a Rockne's restaurant.

"There are witnesses here. Mommy, he can't do anything here."

At the cul-de-sac, his Camaro starts circling Mommy's Audi, centering and lining the driver's window with his gun brandishing and aimed at Mommy's head.

"You think you can get away from me? You'll never get away. You gonna get away from me and the Audi I paid for?" he taunted.

"John, there are people here, families. Would you stop this? I'm done with this. I'm not going to raise my kids in fear."

A grey SUV slowly starts emerging from a parking spot behind John, and an elderly white gentleman peers his head out, yelling, "Hey, is everything all right?" as he blocks John's path to us.

"Get the hell out of here," I heard him start.

Then I shouted, "Mommy, go! Go, the highways right there!"

And she peels away, and we disappear into a cloud of smoke.

CHAPTER 9:

Single Motherhood Move to Wooster

Fresh off the heels of her escape from John, we had moved to some Battered women's shelters in the suburbs before eventually settling down in Wooster, then moving on to Barberton two years later.

Life in Wooster Memory

George Bush vs John Kerry rally in Wooster at thirteen. By then, Faith and I had settled down into life as sixth and then seventh graders at the secluded suburban Cornerstone & Edgewood middle schools.

Our mom insisted we stay up late to watch the boring presidential debates before bed. A Fox News reel pointed out that Bush was wearing a hearing aid in his ear while debating Kerry and, later, unofficial ballot winner Al Gore, who ultimately lost the presidency.

We'd groan, but later on, when the hearing aid incident was turned into a spoof on Saturday Night Live, Faith and I were a hit re-enacting choice parts with mocking voices as the Republicans, making the preps silently bristle with envy, and our party table erupted in laughter.

I have a cute photo of us at the sixth-grade dance that I'll add to the end; we really were a little crew for a minute before my school fight saga began.

At the school dance, everyone stared at us. Faith and I were called the life of the party with Asia, her new boyfriend Avanti from Atlanta, on-off wannabe prep country Sammie, and Valencia, one of the only black girls in our grade, Faith's friend.

We met at the four-square yard, where we *always* dominated, for our developing girl group choir band squad, "Leading Ladies," at Valencia's grandmother Dottie Hampton's church in Wooster. New Revelation church was only the third of three total black churches in the entire city. Compared to ethnic central and southern Warren, Wooster was like night and day. I remember the knee-deep snow swallowing Aunt Ella as she stepped out of her Denali on one of our Thanksgiving "Try the Family Thing" episodes. Faith and I giggled at her petite frame while Uncle Jerry rushed to help her with an infant fox terrier. Spike was iconic for us at thirteen.

"You're not really going to that Bush rally thing this weekend, are you? We still have rehearsal on Sunday," Valencia asked, quickly adjusting her glasses and tossing me the ball.

I caught it and said, "We'll still be there. I'll force my mom, haha. My mom says he's just riding through on a charter bus; we're making John Kerry signs downtown. My mom makes calls getting people to register to vote over the phone. Faith said she wants to go, I think?"

I say quickly, bouncing the ball to Faith. She scuffles to catch it, already out of the four-square bounds, but of course, always fashionably in pink, she's unfazed since there are only three of us.

"Um, yeah! I said I didn't wanna go cuz Mommy's always shoving stupid politics down our throat while we have no cell phone! Anyway, I heard that one redhead girl I had to catch getting in her mom's car with my clothes on is going. I made her take them off and give me the bag; then, I put her in her place. So, I kinda wanna go. To put her in her place again. Don't try to get in my way this time, okay, Jordie?"

I'm growing apprehensive but agree while, of course, not fully confident in her motives.

A huge banner with the political democratic campaigners is roughly two yards long, wishing Kerry personal well wishes and soliloquies of their own. Our anti-Iraqi oil and 9/11 signs are prepared for the day to come.

We march from the top of the hill on Spink Street, six blocks; other supporters join, shouting and jeering, some in trucks with more banners leading the way to downtown. Faith and I think of our cheer parade in Twinsburg, feeling the mile upon us. We eventually passed the Battered Women's Shelter, and we fled from the Maksimovics for sanctuary, feeling even more incensed to speak our chants.

"Bush out now! No more four years!" on repeat, and other impassioned additions.

My mom started screaming, "Yeah! Go send more good young, poor white and black boys to die for your fake war, Bush!" in a growl that startled a group of college boys for a moment, who then continued their chants.

At the sight of the growing Republican crowd across from us in all red, Faith started screaming, "Nobody going to Iraq to die for you racist, broke people!" Feeling her cheeks get hot around Mommy, who gave her a stern look and shoulder pull back.

"Just say the chant now, okay, baby? That's good," she says warmly, and we settle to survey the scene.

Boys with eggs are aiming at the democratic boy's car, and they are fleeing. Some girls are dressed in cheer shirts and looking around nervously.

The towering charter bus approaches, and organizers begin pushing others to the sidewalk where we're standing.

A man in blue face paint screams, "Get ready now! Bush is here!"

The bus approaches slowly and a faint hand and smirk can be seen, the hand looking like a painted glove from my viewpoint, slightly waves, and a group of boys manage to land two eggs at a neighboring window.

Security guards immediately shove them out of view and as a very petite girl myself, I can't see anything but the crowd being shoved to the right side of the street.

I lose sight of my mom and begin to panic, searching through jeering faces, hot and sweaty and enraged. Then suddenly, I see Faith in the alley by the one business that had unfortunately succumbed to vandalism, and Faith screaming at a crowd of laughing girls, shouting, "Haha! Bush is gonna win again!"

I retorted, "Bush dodged the war like a coward! Kerry actually fought for his country, like are you serious?"

To which the ringleader replied, "Get over it! Nobody cares about you anyway; that's why you're really mad, ha-ha!"

To which Faith exploded in anger, screaming, "Are you kidding me? You look dusty! Like, are you serious? You gotta steal clothes I wear cause you're broke as hell and racist! And have the nerve to think you are better than somebody cause you are white? Hahaha, you're a joke!"

At that moment, the girl's burly father lunges, and I jerk toward him, screaming, "Faith, no!" But it's too late.

She's already pummeling the blond girl with a flurry of quick blows. The girl who was whimpering fell backward into a corner near parked cars; the crowd grew even further incensed, and angry screams could be heard everywhere.

I saw some teen boys break Faith off of the girl, and I rushed over to them and grabbed her quickly, yelling, "Faith! Oh my God, get back here now! Are you crazy?"

Suddenly, Mommy is back to my left, with a campaigner guy friend quickly guiding and shielding us with his jacket to his car.

"Yeah, we should definitely get a move on. That guy had to get tackled by three other guys, and they were already about to block off the street with the eggs anyway."

That political rally fight felt like we had fought for a righteous cause, even if the holy fire spilled out over Wooster's streets that day.

From Wooster, Warren Fam Tone–Shift Memory

We would always come to visit our family in Warren for the holidays. Momma Toni had insisted that we try the "family thing" again, and in already knowing the dynamic of our family long before I was born — (the dynamic being, the brains, or the smart people were pathetic losers and the physically strong or athletes were a gift from God) even if they weren't especially religious, that was the notion behind their taunts and cruelty. My mom, in attempts to deflect from prying questions of "Where's John? How's Allie?" When it came time to question her about our academics, she could no longer rest on the suburban cloak of living in a better neighborhood than her once tormentors-turned-family did. She'd start trying to slip "ain'ts" and slang she usually would never say at home, sounding as unnatural and cringey as you could imagine a former teacher turned housewife would sound. The sudden onslaught of slang usage was more so to deflect from our crumbling family situation than to face our family hot seat, so her ploy became to humiliate Faith and me and shift the attention from her own accountability.

"Oh, you know Faith and Jordan are smart like their Momma."

"What about Faith wanting to run track?" our cousin JayJay quipped, quick to turn the conversation back to sports. "Faith ain't running no track; her fast self will be pregnant before she turns eighteen." She smiled wryly and all-knowingly, trying to imitate Aunt

Ella's brash brand of confidence, which also rested on humiliation at the expense of her husband, my uncle JJ.

It was town news and a running joke of how many times my sassy aunt Ella had playfully teased my uncle Jerry, and she openly joked about it in front of us and our hardworking and docile uncle Jerry. He used to either grovel or beg Aunt Ella to change, literally on his knees in front of us kids growing up. Yet, in later years, he would just quietly leave the room as if she wasn't talking about him.

Faith interjected, her face feeling hot, "I'm not gonna get pregnant. I don't know why you keep saying that! I only have had one boyfriend who I met online 'cos you never let us do anything!"

The room fell silent for a minute, and I heard an instigating "oop!" from Aunt Ella and silent snickers from my cousins. "You keep talkin' crazy before you don't have that new computer I just got your ungrateful self. Get out of this kitchen before I whoop your little behind in front of your cousins."

Our cousins hooped and hollered, making a show out of our exit. Faith left in a rush, and I left a little after, hoping my real mother would emerge, but that kitchen was also the same kitchen where Ebert had beaten her with extension cords, so I let her have the moment while, of course, seething on the inside. At not being able to trust or confide in my aunt and uncle, at taking the brunt of Faith's stifled athletic ego, and nursing and caring for my ailing mother while she histrionically zapped my adolescence from me under her web of lies.

My cousin Layla wasn't the favorite like Jalisa was, Jalisa being the high-"yellow bone" golden child, favored strictly for colorism purposes, quietly kept secret. Jalisa and little JJ were afforded all of the extracurriculars (cheerleading, football, and basketball came to them first, the younger three after). Even in their own family, they had favoritism. Layla's claim to fame came when Aunt Ella became a basketball coach at her high school, and she was also on the track team. One night, Faith and Layla raced in front of everyone at Aunt Ella's, and even barefoot and doubted, Faith dusted Layla in that race, showing the potential she had while being untrained. So, for Faith to be begrudged in her track racing, even while still agreeing to be homeschooled, was the nail in the coffin for our homestead in Barberton.

CHAPTER 11:

Barberton & Cousins Memory

Once we had moved on from Wooster, Faith and I joined the choir in Barberton, to try and make some friends. We were officially baptized together at Liberty Baptist Church, when we were sixteen in the basement. Their new church was in the works, being built in the countryside of Barberton.

A few of my cousins from my other aunt Sharon came to visit Faith and me in Barberton that July. Their visit came a few months before our Halloween party that we had, even though we were strict Christians. I really don't know why our mom insisted on the Halloween party; I think it was to compete with Ella because Jalisa was having some kind of majorette party.

Anyway, my cousins Dani, Tariq, and Adrian came to visit us at Lake Anna in Barberton.

Tariq said, "Dang, this is nice. But don't y'all get bored out here, all these old white people?"

I was immediately annoyed with him always bringing race into it, but I was determined for them to have a good visit and report to bring back, so I said, "Macy and Spike need to go out; let's go walk around the Lake. Bring some bread to feed the ducks."

Tariq and Adrian seemed to like chasing the ducks, with baby beagle Macy and our noble fox terrier Spike on their leashes, herding the flock along. Then, seeing our library hangout. "At least you can get on MySpace, I guess," Tariq muttered under his breath before we walked out. Eventually, they left because they needed to go home for their basketball game.

But Dani wanted to stay, and she stayed with us for about a week, and it was really great. We were away from the other influences in Warren, and we could really connect.

First was our stop to save a lot in the Barberton Plaza.

Dani said, "We're just gonna go in here like Aunt Net, or I mean your mom was outside in the car waiting for us, but we're gonna say, oh hi, our EBT card outside, then dip! Come on, y'all." She squealed, and in a flash, she was off, grabbing a cart, saying, "Just those things right dere, these crackers, slim Jims, fish sticks," slamming them into the cart laughing. She said, "Come on. Ooh and lemme get these yams."

Faith started joining like, "Oh, I need some hair bows, and I need these little sunglasses too, and I don't even know what this is, but, yeah, put it in the cart!" behind giggles.

I reluctantly joined in, "That's not on EBT, so I hope you have some money." I started joining in and tossed in some frozen meals. "Some of these hungry men, 'Dang, I'm hungry, man,'" I said, exaggeratingly laughing, and we all dashed to the register, ready to play out our prank.

"Oh, oh, our mom has an EBT card; we gotta go outside to get it," Dani stammered through pursed lips, fighting back laughs, and we hurriedly ran out of the store into the Fashion Bug fitting rooms laughing. In the corner of our eye, we could see the bewildered cashier standing next to the cart spilling over with frozen dinners, chips, and sodas.

The next day of Dani's visit, Faith and I decided to go to the Lake Anna flowerbeds.

We had waterskied with Barberton High, still agreeing to be homeschooled, and did face painting for kids at the Cherry Blossom Festival. Faith and I were also modeling scouts at sixteen for Barbizon modeling, an audition I had secretly enrolled us into, that later our cousin Dani got to witness our practiced top model catwalk during Barbizon's orientation week the following week.

That day on Lake Anna had us running from Lake Anna to the flowerbeds, and we loved the flowers so much one time we actually dug up a few of the flowers and then would run to our house and then like plant them and go back-and-forth doing that.

We only did that one time, but apparently, someone saw us because we were only like fourteen or fifteen around this time and called the police on us.

Our mom was working in her room and didn't even know it was a police officer knocking on the door, hissing lowly, "I'm on the phone. And if it's the landlord, pretend I'm not here!" and we were hiding and giggling, it was super hilarious that even our mom was an accomplice to our flower banditry.

Then Dani came up with a new idea, "Let's do prank calls! It's so boring I don't see how y'all can be homeschooled."

Faith chimed in, "You know we're not being homeschooled by choice. Our mom wants us to stay home because she needs us to help with her fibromyalgia. We already told you this, and anyways, let's just do prank calls."

Dani started and said, "Let's do one across the street; they are having a party." So we grabbed the phone book and started going down the list.

"Wait before you call. Press the star signal; it looks like the little snowflake, then sixty-nine, that will block the call so they can't find it. Because if you don't, the police will be here again, and not for flowers," Danni said.

She was like, "Oh, Pizza Hut." Then, she said, "Hello, Pizza Hut? Hold on just a sec."

At that moment, she put her hand over the phone's receiver, whispering to us, and said, "Quick, think of a number between one and fifty that sounds real."

"Like forty? Forty-seven?" Faith chimed in.

I said, "No, that's way too much. Um, what about like twenty?"

Dani says, "No, that's not enough. Twenty-seven. Hello, Pizza Hut. Hello. Okay, hey, I'm back. Yo, I need like twenty-seven pizzas! We are having a party! Put it with anchovies on it, and I need that ASAP. We have like forty people over; it's crazy!" in an exciting DJ voice, and Faith and I were stifling laughter, reveling at her bravery.

Then we just couldn't contain it anymore, and I was whispering, "Faith, go play music so it sounds like a lot of people are here."

Then Danielle was like, "Oh yeah, yeah, I need twenty-seven pizzas. Anchovies only, and cheese, of course."

The boy on the phone was like, "Twenty-seven pizzas? Are you serious? Do you know how long that's going to take? Hold on a sec."

He came back five minutes later and said, "Boss said we can actually have that done for you in about three hours, so what's your address?"

We gave him the address from across the street, and then we were like, "Oh my God, thank you so much; you're a lifesaver!" We clicked the phone off and died of laughter for I don't even know how long.

Next, it was Faith's turn, but she couldn't think of a good place to call. She said, "Let's just call like old random people in the phonebook." So she found this one number, and she just kept calling each number that she would go down and see who answered.

She called one guy, and he angrily and kind of gruffly answered "hello," and she got into character saying, "Why did you cheat on me? Why did you cheat on me — " glancing at the phonebook, "um, D-David! See, that's why you're mad; why do you answer the phone all irritated?"

The guy said, without missing a beat, "I didn't cheat on you. You know I didn't. Wait, who is this? Is this Donna? This, this better not be Don — " and then we quickly hung up the phone, and our stomachs were hurting from laughter.

Macy sauntered in and started laying on the rug, patiently waiting for pets and then Dani turned to me, "Your turn, Jordie."

I thought for a minute, like, okay, what's gonna sound convincing?

Just then, Dani grabbed the phone and dialed a random number; an angry, gruff man's voice answered, bellowing, "Who the heck is this?"

She screamed, "Dave Chappelle!" and then banged on the phone, clicking the receiver with Faith and her cracking up into bouts of laughter while beagle Macy was trying to get in on the fun, and I still had to come up with a place to call.

Then thought back to the long chore list my mom had scribbled on a bill, that I had done while Faith haughtily ignored it for the umpteenth time. So, I decided to call a nursing home.

I had been complaining about my mom being kind of overprotective all day, so I pretended to be grown even though I was fifteen, and I tried my best grown woman voice before I called.

I practiced a British accent but settled on a really exaggerated southern accent that was cracking Faith and Dani up and went to town.

I started off with, "Hello, hello. Hello? Lady, hello. Okay. I really need to speak to somebody that can get this old lady out of my house. Cause she don't clean, she don't cook, she don't do nothing. But boss people around twenty-four-eight, and I can't deal, okay?"

I heard Dani let out a funny snort, and Faith buried her face in the pillow, but I kept going.

A soft-spoken, nice lady's voice came on the other end of the line, "Oh. Ehrm. Hello, ma'am. Well, I am sorry that this is happening. I'm sorry you're going through this. Wait, what did you say your name was?"

I had to think on the spot, so I remember I just made up something like, "Oh, I'm Dolores, Steinbeck, and this ole lady need to get in check. I'm trying to tell you."

"Okay, okay, calm down. Well, we do have a lot of good amenities here for your…. You said your grandmother, right?" she asked shakily.

"My mother, yes. It's like she has arthritis. Girl, she has everything under the sun, and what she don't have is manners, child. And I can't deal. Cuz you can't be about to die but still act like you about to be King Kong in here!"

I had to bury my face in the pillow at that point because laughter bubbled up inside me, and I gave the phone to Faith for a minute.

"Hello, ma'am? Ma'am, are you still there? Okay, I hear you're having some issues in your home and we do have some great amenities here for your mother, you said. How old is she?"

"Girl, she seventy-two 'n a half years old, I don't know how she still alive, but yeah, but."

"Oh, um, okay, so seventy-two years old. That's nice. We have some senior lap pool facilities for that age group, which really helps with the arthritic issues."

Just then, my mom barged in the door and was yelling.

"Come get these groceries out of the car! You didn't hear me leaning on the horn for the past ten minutes?"

I was still on the tail end of my little performance when she barged in the room saying that, and she heard me. She heard me saying, "Yes, I hope she cud have a room. I hope yaw cud deal with her 'cos I'm tired of taking care of this lady. She dead weight!" to the laughter of Danielle and Faith, and then the blood immediately draining from my face at seeing my mom there.

I turned to see her startled, then at the swing, Dani's laughter saying, "Oh, yeah. Haha, that's really funny. Come on, help," but there was still a little twinge of uneasiness in her voice.

I never realized how much those joking moments were actually more so premonitions of what was to come in the future.

CHAPTER 12 :

Home Life in Barberton — the Beginning of the End of our Homestead

Faith and I kept a diary to document the various moves we went through and to remember what we said or how we truly felt without our family manipulating and twisting the narrative. In comparing our diaries, I can see how we both were scrambling to put the drama at home into perspective. To understand how things had ended up so horribly wrong and the kind of life that had spurred it on.

Faith's Diary — March 18th, 2008

Dear Lord,

This is a continued one because while I wrote the 17th and 18th on the same day, I needed to fill it up, and I'm still confiding in You. I want to wait until I've filled more lines to tell You what's on my mind. Well, I guess here is as good as it gets, sigh. My cell phone keeps binging for some reason, and it's annoying me. Lol, but that's not my problem.

Well, last night, I looked up tips for, I guess, pleasuring myself because I just wasn't pleasing myself, so I looked up tips, but when I tried, this unnatural thing came to me all on its own, and it's the first time I realized why people enjoy doing it, but I also read that you may feel dirty after and they mentioned that most girls do, but it's nothing to be ashamed of yadda, yadda, yadda. I already knew that because God gave people pleasure spots, it must not be wrong since You invented it. Oh, but there goes that dumb cell phone again, lol. I'll have to wait and see what it beeping for, anyway. The truth is I only felt dirty like that for a second, and then it went away.

Here is an odd thing, though. One girl, or maybe it was a woman, mentioned her being really sleepy afterward, and I was too. I was wide awake in the beginning, but suddenly, I found myself drowsy later. Anyway, I also felt really energized, and I do right now. For some reason, after, you feel this surge of energy like you could run a mile. For some reason, God, You made that happen.

Well, anyway, speaking of energy, please give me enough energy to get to the why and strengthen my back and legs if I think I have any hope of trying track. In the name of Jesus, I pray. Amen. Well, at least it starts in April the conditioning, so I still have time. Also, Lord, please help me study hard and get more tests done. Only with Your help can I. In the name of Jesus, I pray. Amen.

Well, the cell phone stopped beeping, lol. That was getting annoying. Oh, yeah, God, thank You for letting me meet those nice new girls at the Cavs game with that youth group. Which, by the way, was really fun. We all screamed our little hearts out for everything, lol, including for Sasha of The Cave and Brady Quinn, a fine player of the Browns; he and Sasha were fine! Lol, and it was also, of course, good to see LeBron James. It was a really cool game and a really fun night overall. Thank You, Jesus. Well, now I'm going to take a shower and get cracking on my schoolwork. Thank You for everything, God.

Love, Faith.

Dear God,

Yeah, I'm writing You right now because I forgot to write You in the past several days, and I seriously need to get back on that. Well, first off, I just wanted to say I love You and thank You for my blessings and the blessings You've given Mommy. Thanks to those talks I had with Mommy on Saturday while picking up soul food in the car and the talk I had after we all ate and watched 200 cigarettes about the annoying and nagging Levi situation and everything else, too. Thank You for giving her the right words to say so I could see clearly and let my mind be on the right track.

I am no longer in that desperate need of a boyfriend, and now it seems realistic to wait rather than be tempted to have sex because that's most likely to happen if I just picked any old unsaved boy. My mind is no longer consumed by the thoughts of what could have been and what should have been because the point is I broke it off, and God told me, well, You told me to. I'm glad I listened; otherwise, I'd probably be pregnant by now because of his desperate wanting for a family.

I still do miss him as a friend and hope that, God, if it's Your will, we can be again someday. Well, I apologize again for not writing You for the though so many days; You deserve much more than what I do. I know You forgive me, but please help me make more of a conscious effort to write You. It prevents fights with Jordan and also brings me closer to You. Thank You that I live in a country that enables me to do that.

Faith's Diary — March 26, 2008

Dear Lord,

Well, I'm writing this in reference to yesterday because I hadn't written You. Well, yesterday was okay except for my yelling, but I was only trying to be heard because Mommy never lets me get a word in. Ha, I apologized, and all she said was okay. I always forgive her, so whatever, anyway.

I was mad at Jordan that day because I thought she was making up all her problems. Because, as You know, on the 19th, she started this big, long feud with Mommy. Mommy claimed Jordan punched her, but even though I didn't see it, it didn't sound like Jordan had hit her at all. Also, when she was holding her down on the couch, she said Jordan was kicking her in the back when what I saw was Jordan's legs in front of her own body and her squirming away. Also, I was mad at her because she started all that drama that night by saying really mean things to her and disrespectful and appalling things that I never thought she would ever say, so as You know, Mommy called the cops, and they came.

They took Jordan to juvie, and the next day, I had to go to court with Mommy. It was weird. I was tired, angry, and upset and trying to keep Mommy strong because if I was weak, then she'd definitely fall apart because she's already so fragile as it is.

Jordan came in some weird outfit with shackles in court and her hair a mess, and I was in shock and stunned and everything. Long story short, she ended up staying again because I didn't think she was ready to come home because she didn't even seem appreciative, and I believed Momma's story about what happened because Jordan was so obviously out of control, so she came home a day later because she was too crazy for safe landing. She went to Children's.

I was, I guess, in shock that she would do this all over again. But later on, I realized that Jordan and I had lived half our lives under constant stress about where we would live, food, money, etc. So that and losing loved ones that you can never get back, so it's just a lot of stress and depression and also me putting her through hell when we were isolated and miserable, so all of that build-up anger and stress finally let out.

She's been through counseling at Children's Hospital. I saw her yesterday; she's normal again. Thank You, Jesus. Lol. And she should be here soon, so I still have stress, and thinking about Levi is the only way I can release it nowadays, my only joy or strength or anything. Personal counselors are coming Saturday for me, and Jordan Patty, our youth group leader, came with McDonald's the day before yesterday to help and comfort me. So, hopefully, I can get some counseling, too, so I can deal with my annoying, insane mother, who likes to call me the B word if I say something in the slightest attitude.

One thing I will agree with Jordan is when she said that she's too sensitive about everything. Because it's true! She is. I'm so tired of her always talking about sad things in the past and feeling sorry for herself even though she says she doesn't, but she does. I constantly have to hear about her stupid sickness, her stupid job, her stupid boss! Her, her, her! all the time. And if I say one little stupid thing wrong or with a slight annoyance, then I'm my crazy father or even the B word or an ungrateful brat. Then, two seconds later, she tries to talk to me like she didn't say anything; she has serious issues, and I wish I could get away from her and stop constantly massaging her stupid, weak body; it doesn't even barely help. That's enough, so bye. Faith.

Faith's Diary — March 27th, 2008

Dear Lord,

So fast forward to Easter, which was the 25th. We had a late start because Mommy was sick (but we were more dressed up and ready), so we waited patiently. Jordan wrote to the girls in juvie. I did little notings in MySpace; she got ready finally, and we took pics and left.

We were supposedly going to a Chinese restaurant, but it was closed. So, after a long deliberation, we decided on Red Lobster. Yeah, it's not exactly the fanciest place ever, but it was nice enough. We played word games, ate, took a few pictures, and had fun. Recognized the guy from an old church, and then she wanted to see *The Other Boleyn Girl*, but we really wanted to see *There Will Be Blood*, so she reluctantly agreed to see it. So, we bought time at Barnes and Noble.

She had originally wanted to go to this church service at a church we'd never been to, but we didn't. We saw *There Will Be Blood*; it was great, but she hated it. She said it was boring, with no dialogue, when it was extremely entertaining, made you think, and was very original.

So, anyway, a day after Easter, we had started this convo about God and purity yadda, yadda, yadda. I was sad and missing you-know-who and felt like I would never find a boyfriend. Mommy said good things that helped me, and then I agreed with what she was saying, and then Jordan thought I was taking her side, and then it erupted into this long, draining thing where Jordan was acting the same way she had on the 19th (when she was arrested). She went to bed. Mommy was mad because she had told her chores to do, and Jordan didn't do them, but she didn't care anyway until the fight happened.

Long story short, Mommy told Jordan to get up and ask her questions, and Jordan was annoyed, mean, and disrespectful all over again, and she was going to be sent to a place called Safe Landing. But Jordan thought it would be like juvie and really threw a fit, screaming on the floor, etc. Mommy was forced to call the cops.

After this and then she had to go to the hospital, I guess,
and then I had to endure this long talk between Mommy and
Jordan. Like, 'Yes, you did do this' and 'No, you didn't say
that,' blah blah blah. So Jordan finally admitted that she was
sorry and wrong. So then after she told me about girls she met
in juvie and the mean guards, I just thought it was so weird
she was there. We watched **She's the Man**, *and everything*
was seemingly okay. Jordan also acknowledged that she was
restricted from all phones, computers, etc.

Well, that's all for now I'll continue next.
Love, Faith.

Jordan's Diary — August 5th, 2008

So now that I've told you all that, which wasn't as painful as I
thought it would be, I'll finally tell you the rest of what led up
to us being put in foster care. I told my mom I had a new test
to take that day, and she replied, "Well, you'll have to go to the
library because I'm taking the cord."

Confused, I asked, "Why when I can just take it here?"
Now, looking back, I realized that she probably did it
because I had a little tone when I told her I had a new test. A
wrong look or gesture is enough to set her off into hysterics or
whatever. She also warned that she was going to start to do
things "differently" if we continued to act like demonic brats.
I admit that sometimes I was just outright disrespectful and
rude to her as well as Faith. We didn't know where all the
anger was coming from until we realized that she was the
reason for all the pain and anguish we had experienced in our
lives.

So, she said, "If you don't like it, you can walk up to the
library or get out of my house."

Upset that she was being so mean to me, I said, "We had it yesterday and only used it for schoolwork, so I don't know why you're taking it away!" So she ignored me and went to take the computer cord and get her purse for work. I stomped downstairs and said, "It seems like you like punishing us."

She screamed for me to "get yourself upstairs," and I knew that meant a spanking, so I grabbed the broom and yelled, "I don't deserve a whoopin' for this; leave me alone."

She pushed me back against the wall and started jerking me all around, telling me to look at her, grabbing my head and banging it on the wall, screaming, "I said look at me," while pulling my hair.

Every time she started one of these "look at me!" things, she hit us in the face when we didn't expect it. I refused, so she pushed me into my room and started pounding on my back as I curled up into a ball. For some reason, even though I knew she was really wrong, I didn't have the audacity to hit her back in self-defense. She's my mother, and I can never do that despite what she thinks.

Well, my sister, who was in the shower and dreading getting out hearing us fighting, came into the room in a robe, shouting, "What are you doing? Get off her."

My mom ignored her and continued wailing at me. Faith rushed to the phone and called her counselors, who were already scheduled to come that day anyway. My mom had set us up with counselors because she did this weird thing where she'd switched from abusive mom to loving, nurturing, caring mom.

Jordan's Diary — August 10th, 2008

So, our counselors came along with the police because my mom wanted to tell them her made-up version about how both

Faith and I attacked her and get us into juvie for six months. Luckily, our counselors defended us and got us out of that crazy situation, and now, three foster homes and one group home later, this is where we are.

Each day is a challenge in a different way. One is to not go off on some of these kids like Chase and Delicia are two especially annoying cases, and to not die of boredom or longing for the outside world. I miss MySpace so badly. I think about my last profile, which I hardly remember because I uploaded it on my last day of freedom. My sister reassured me that it was cute during one of our brief, rare phone calls because she'd seen it before she left.

Anyway, I'm not getting any more time packed on; I'm staying here for only three months; any more than that will be too much to bear, and I might just lose it as I did at that other cottage place in this little community of crazy kid buildings freedom is going to taste so sweet right now seeing as I don't have any guys who care about me I'm going to I guess crush on some of these cute stuff guys that work here.

Despite our mother's strict rules on dating, Faith persisted and challenged my mother's rules of "Well, you can date… but only if I'm in the room."

"Okay then," Faith would say defiantly. "Then I want him to come over so you can meet him," and she grudgingly agreed.

A memory of one sunny afternoon when he had come to visit Faith after school, he confided to us about how his mother had died when he was very young, and he was adopted by his aunt, but that how it "never really felt like home" to him. When I asked why he was already thinking of having kids at such a young age, he said, "I want to start a family and give my child the love I didn't have growing up," and images of Faith in a white dress filled my head, and I beamed with joy thinking of what a beautiful bride Faith would be.

I remember Levi bringing his friend Clarence over and my mom renting *American Gangster* with Denzel Washington and all of us watching it with my mom keeping a close eye on Faith and Levi, cuddled at the far end of the couch next to her.

Levi was about to turn eighteen and planned to join the military from what Faith told me, but my mom was more so worried about the fact that he had come from a broken home and had his heart set on starting a new family. He wanted the fairytale with Faith, who was a mystery to him. They'd spend hours talking on the phone, and much to my surprise, Faith didn't become mush like me in front of attractive boys, at the time, being sheltered and homeschooled at sixteen. Despite our isolation, Faith was confident and firm in her personality and made Levi earn every laugh and every smidgen into her life. Sometimes, on Instant Messenger, Levi would email me and ask me what I could do to get Faith to open up to him. I'd send a laughing emoji and tell him to keep working his way into her life slowly like he had been and not rush her because she could easily cut people off from her emotions. Sometimes, our chats would become lengthy, and Faith would get suspicious, so I would keep them short, but even though a part of me longed to be desired in the way that Levi yearned for Faith, I felt a sisterly honor in being able to preserve Faith's innocence and mystique and that overrode any sense of lack in me.

CHAPTER 13:

Halloween Party Memory

One time, due to Faith's persistence and even overt rebellions where she'd burst with anger at my mother after one of her unwarranted and depressing recollections of her childhood, exclaiming, "We're not your therapists! We're kids! Don't you think we've had enough of taking in all the horrible abuse stories from you? That's why our family hates us, and it's all your fault! Yeah, our dad may not have been in our lives, but the *one* time we did meet him at his mom's funeral, and he wanted to write to us and have us visit, *you* blocked it and cut him off! You never gave him a chance!" She'd cry as if the words were a bubbling volcano inside of her that had been dying to come out. I sat in silent reverence at her bravery but winced as I dreaded the backlash.

Times where I had chosen to side with her would result in extra chores as punishment for co-signing Faith, while Faith would not be penalized.

My mom would go from morose to a cold and sullen and dark voice I didn't recognize, saying, "Yeah! I know I cut him off for a reason! To protect you from his insanity. Did you know when your sperm donor was a kid, he would sexually harass your aunt Deedee?" She'd cry out hysterically to the deep groans and growls of Faith, rightfully exasperated at these recollections of events neither one of us was alive for.

"Mommy, why don't you ever try therapy?" I'd ask quietly, trying to add reason to the building chaos. "We may be smart, but we're still only teenagers. Maybe if you got these feelings out — " but I'd always be cut off, seen as the weaker vessel for her to put into submission.

"You think me talking to some rich uppity white person who's getting *paid* to listen to my problems is gonna help anything? No."

Yet one day, in a recycled episode of this same argument, my mom surprised us.

"Fine. You say I don't let you do anything, then fine. You can have a Halloween party. It's not demonic if we aren't worshipping Satan, so don't start with me. So fine. Invite some of your old friends from Wooster, Candace, and Chasidy and some of your friends online, and we'll have it."

"The fact that we have to drudge up friends from seventh grade because we have none is pathetic," Faith would say, unimpressed by my mother's efforts.

I felt the same way, but as the time drew nearer and nearer — and I started making flyers for the party, inviting some of my local friends I had made to the party — we both couldn't help but get excited. Mommy had to physically drive to Wooster and get my old friends whom I hadn't seen in years, and we all decorated our living room; the sliding doors bordered in mahogany wood became streamers of the undead, and my mom found motion activated Frankensteins to spook passerbys. When I had asked Faith who she had invited, she said, "It looks like all the boys on here who had crushes on us are coming. Great. Our party is gonna be five girls and like thirty guys. Ugh."

The Halloween party day had finally arrived, and sure enough, boys from all corners of Akron were pouring in. To my surprise, many of them knew of me even though they were Faith's friends. Mommy had on her silly oversized pimp hat and was hard at work in the steamy kitchen whipping up tacos and going in to chaperone the boys in the living room and bring out entrees and plates to keep the rowdy kids occupied.

A new friend I met, Sonya, who was actually twelve but had lied and told me she was fourteen, joined us — Faith, Chasidy, Candace, and I — as we ran upstairs, giggling and shyly hiding from the boys.

Faith had on her pink cowgirl hat and brown boots, and I was fixing my weave ponytail I brought out for special occasions, saying I was a disco girl of sorts, none of us really wanting to fully commit to the costume idea that in our mature age of sixteen seemed "lame."

Eventually, I begged them to join me downstairs because I saw some of the boys starting to fight over "who got which twin." It was terrifying for me to think of my jubilant mom being in the midst of a crowd of angry and restless boys. I whipped out our karaoke machine we had gotten from Big Lots and tried to make the scene cool by picking one of the only hip-hop songs the system had to offer. Clarence jumped up to help me and started rapping over the Usher "Caught Up" song with me, to the delight of everyone in the room and my mom, of course, stepping in with her scene-stealing-moment of jokes that put everyone at ease.

As I was laughing, I remember my mom yoking me up briefly and hissing in my ear, "Stop showing off and shaking your little fast behind in front of all these boys, dummy. Go get the camera I bought where the ghosts will show up on film. You know where it is — don't start with me. Change that tight dress, too." I sighed deeply at the moment of joy being snatched from me. "And you better wipe that attitude and tone out of your voice when I'm talking to you!"

I ran upstairs and changed into a tee shirt and jeans and ran back down. Chasidy had started to loosen up and formed a line dance and organized everyone to start dancing to the popular Soulja Boy "Do the Stanky Leg, Do the Stanky Leg" dance, much to my relief at keeping the crowd entertained; I was glad everyone seemed to be having a good time. My mom began beckoning everyone around for various photo ops. I saw Levi and Clarence strike a cool pose, and then Chasidy whipped around quickly for a photo next to a very sullen and obstinate me, still taken aback at my mom's underlying harshness. I wish I could've faked it for that photo, but I wanted to remember why I hadn't smiled in it once it was developed.

Watching my mom's headlights slowly shrink away from the foster care group home snaps me out of the flooding memories and reminded me that I wasn't there at all; I was here.

CHAPTER 14:

How Faith and I Entered Foster Care

Our caseworker Karen pulled up with Faith and me in front of a beige house with dark shutters, a white picket fence, and a wraparound patio in the back.

"This is P.A.L. Mission Girl's Home. It'll be a good place for you girls. You'll be able to learn job skills and even get scholarships for college. But these people are very strict. If you don't follow the rules and work their program, they will kick you out. It'll be a nice change of pace for you. What with your overbearing mother, she got off the phone with me not too long ago and said she had to sell one of your dogs. I'm sorry, girls."

Faith and I cried for a while before entering, thinking of our diva beagle Macy, so used to us painting her nails, buying her baby clothes from Goodwill, and making her outfits, her proud floppy ears when she'd pin a squirrel at the lake, now probably so scared and upset with us suddenly being gone.

"The day we called children services, our mom was first serving the counselors lemonade then cursing at us, calling us smuts even though we're a virgin, throwing shoes at us, saying we were ungrateful brats and gonna get molested by some old, overweight guy; don't tell me anything she says!" Faith grumbled to our counselor.

I reminded her, "You were the one that called children's services, our counselors, on Mommy, and yeah. So quit saying we. Because you called them. She was spanking me with the bareback broom, spanking me like always, over our Penn Foster online homework she barely graded. Whatever, and you made it worse by screaming, 'Get off of her,'" I said mockingly. "Then, even after I asked you over and over, you still said you wanted to go!"

Faith cut me off, saying annoyedly, "I know! Hell, no, I don't wanna stay with her. She sent me to Safe Landing just for banging on the bathtub, then sent you to Children's Hospital for cutting, and she's always sending people somewhere for no reason! She had the audacity to send both of us to juvie on Dan Street. For like a week for what? Not washing the baseboards right, like forget her."

Our caseworker gave us some water bottles to wipe our faces off with. "All right, Faith, that's enough. I understand, girls. Let's please just try to make a good first impression."

We collected ourselves and stepped hesitantly into what was to be our new home.

There at the wood oak brown table stood the house director Marissa, two assistants, and three foster girls. A brunette girl named Lauren, a mousy-haired dirty blonde named April, and a masculine-looking red-headed girl, Nellie, always in flannel.

"Welcome, girls. I understand you two are twins! Well, you're just in time for the beginning of the school year in September. For now, follow Lauren and April's lead, and you'll do just fine here," Marissa said, glancing at her clipboard. "Just know that we welcome you with open arms if you follow the rules."

Faith rolled her eyes and briefly sighed at the desperate pleas from me to compose herself, which got Marissa more incensed.

"We don't give out endless chances. Ask April. April, when you got pregnant on your home pass, we kicked you out for a while, didn't we?"

April blushed and peered her head from behind the grandfather clock, saying, "Yeah. They kicked me out for a year. Had to get my guardian at litem to practically beg me back into the program, haha. They're just really big on chores."

"And rules. And respect," Marissa said. "Respect us, and we will respect you."

Later that day, we all piled into the minivan to take Lauren to work.

"Lauren's been here a year and already has management skills at work," the assistant staff lady Courtney said approvingly, behind a sip of green tea, while Marissa drove.

"Bye, losers! Time for me to go make money!" Lauren said and hopped out right in step with a fellow coworker.

I silently envied her freedom as she sauntered off.

Then we stopped at the mall. "Let's just see if there's something affordable in here, girls. Little detour," Courtney said, giving us a wink and making me excited; she may be the fun staffer for sure.

Faith rolled her eyes in irritation. "Wish we didn't have to go to the mall with them. We don't even know them. And they don't have the same taste. They probably think UGG boots and leggings are better than Macy's," she said with a haughty kind of scoff that made me smirk at first, then feel bad as I saw Marissa and Courtney's expressions.

"I could really go for a soda," April said, and the ladies went off.

Faith and I eased our way into Steve and Barry's, and I told Faith, "I'll get you something if you promise to be good."

And I swiped a couple of coral bracelets from the shelf behind a tee shirt, pretending to look at the price while scratching the barcode off and slipping them into my purse before the ladies came back.

"How do you do that, gahhh!" Faith grumbled, slightly happy at her new gift but also slightly jealous that she didn't really have the nerve to pull it off.

A rebellious habit I had picked up with my old friend Asia in Wooster, along with occasionally smoking her mom's cigarettes with her, rebelling due to the harsh bullying going on back then.

"Come on, girls, we gotta get this preggo girl home!" Courtney called out, and we were on our way.

Next, we went to April's place, who was petitely five months pregnant, and we visited her new apartment. Her place was up at least two flights of steps in a quiet wooden apartment. It was the height of July, though, and we felt all like we were stifled for air as we looked at her makeshift crib and nursery for her impending baby girl.

Wow, I guess they really do help these girls, I thought.

Our bedroom was a bright, sunlit room with a white carpet, farm-style furniture, and a huge closet. A few steps down to the other bedroom, with an en suite bathroom and pink curtains.

Faith seemed to like it, too.

"See, Faith? We can make this work. Here's your bracelet. Shhh. Now be good, ya little pear face." Pear face and apple face were our kid nicknames we gave each other growing up, and she chuckled at the remark.

As we were getting settled in and used to our new life, I decided to go sit on the porch and get acquainted.

The other girls seemed to avoid Nellie, the "butch girl," as they called her, but I wasn't into it. I've just never been into ganging up on someone just for the sake of it, and I noticed she was sitting alone. I decided not to just write her off and enjoy some cool dusk air.

"Hey. It's kinda peaceful out here, huh? Mind if I join ya?" I said, pulling up a patio chair.

"Yeah, sure. My bad, I was on the phone cussing out my boyfriend," she said with a sweaty wipe of red hair from her face. "I'm gonna beat him up when I get back to Canton. But I'm stuck in east bum Egypt."

"Oh, wow. Sounds dramatic," I muttered, not wanting to say too much, wishing I had a cigarette, feeling the stress of my rapidly changing life, and looking at the twinkling night sky.

"Yeah, he's like a hot jock but always wants to hide me, ugh. Ha, he'd actually like you a lot. He'd *love* you, actually. He looks like Channing Tatum. While I'm a gremlin," she said woefully.

"Oh no, you're not," I started, but she cut me off.

"Oh, please. I know what I am. But yeah, he'd love you. And your big tits — haha, sorry, couldn't help it."

"I'm a D cup at seventeen, I get it." I chuckled. "My doctor in Wooster actually told me I needed to get breast reduction surgery at thirteen. I was scared to death; I didn't go through with it. But now I have a slight scoliosis from it. Life's crazy."

She chuckled along, saying, "I can def relate; I mean, duhh." She gestured at her own broad chest.

I decided to go in and later told Faith in our spacious shared room. "Yeah, she's not that bad. She's a little different, but she's like a rocker type. She said her boyfriend would like me, which was kind of weird. But other than that, I mean, she seems okay."

"Yeah, I guess. She seems weird," Faith said with a huff and was off to sleep.

In the next week or so, we received our weekly charts and chore schedules; the chores rotated every week.

I vacuumed the living room, hid from staff ladies on the phone, and signed Faith's initials next to it.

CHAPTER 15:

My Diary Entry, October 12th, 2008

Dear diary, after this month we'll finally be three months. Every second feels like an hour, every hour like a day, every day like a week. As you could have guessed, a lot has happened. For one, I'm disowning Faith. Yeah, my own twin. A month or so ago, we had a meeting at a McDonald's with our mom, and I was still in my disgusting uniform. Faith had permed her hair, which our mom had warned us not to do because our hair is soft and fragile. It broke off as she said, but it looked okay, I guess. It was almost shoulder-length. She had on a cute top and nice jeans, earrings, and makeup. Whereas I had my uncombed hair and stupid uniform but was still happy to see my family after so long.

My mom looked at her hair with sadness, and Faith jerked away at her touch. She was so cold and heartless, staring at my mom like she could barely stand her presence.

"Why do you look so fat?" was the first thing she said to me. I was wearing a thick gray-colored shirt and tan dress pants. I had no hair products, so my hair was a poofy mess. Then she started ranting and raving at my mom in public like a maniac. You don't know Faith, so you couldn't possibly imagine an argument with her. I'll tell you a little about what it was like to be trapped in the house with her.

"Hey, Faith, you've been on the computer for like three hours now. Can I get on for like five minutes?"

"Um, no. Go away now, please. Thank you."

"Well, I guess I can get on in a few minutes."

"You can wait until I'm ready to get off. Go away, freak."

"But I —"

"I said go away, now! Ugh! Pa-the-tic. Lou-zer! Go away! And you wonder why I hate you go! Dang!" she starts plugging her ears and yelling this to the top of her lungs.

"I'm sorry, I was just trying," I stammer.

"I don't care!" Faith screams. "Get out of my face, pathetic freak!"

I sighed deeply, and with tears welling up, I just walked away.

That's her on a Tuesday. Even now, while in independent living. We shared two joint bedrooms; our routine was to turn on the radio when we woke up to pump ourselves up. I wake up first and try to wake her up, but she hits me out of nowhere, so I wait a little while, then turn on the radio lowly.

While I'm showering, she bursts open the door, rips the radio out of the wall, crashes it to the floor, and starts banging on the shower door. I wearily got out and started being pushed and kicked for turning on the radio while she was sleeping.

A few days before, she woke me up, and I told her I really wasn't in the mood for music that morning, and she said, "So what? Quit being lazy and get up." Then she blasted the music and even got complaints from the staff about it. I told her I'd do the same thing to her, and all she said was, "So?" so I did.

Instead of accepting it, she went off; I begged her to keep her voice down, "Please, Faith! If you keep yelling, they're gonna kick you out! I'm begging you!"

Faith scoffed. "Uhg, can you stop saying please like that? God! You sound pathetic! Bye, dumb freak. Okay? Thank you."

Another time, she cursed me out because after she told me not to wake her up anymore, so I didn't. I wake up to Faith screeching, "You're so inconsiderate! Oh my God, I hate you! You can forget you have a sister! Forget you have a twin! Cause I'm never talking to you again!"

Even staff outside looking in said she was hopeless and I'd be better off without her craziness. She always clung to me, though, in social situations because she was too snooty to really make herself available or outgoing when it was time for us to make friends the few times we did try at public school.

She called me two weeks after our visit with our mom and cursed me out for wanting to go home. She wants to be independent and says she loves her new life even though she pays no bills, so how can she be independent? Unlike me, she can wear makeup and jewelry, doesn't have a school dress code, and she gets to flirt with boys. I'm so tired of being here; it's not helping at all. I kind of want to cut myself so badly, but I promised God and my mom that I wouldn't. I have no right.

Later that night, "the butch girl" Nellie called me out on it.

As we were all setting the table for dinner, we heard Nellie coming out of the tail end of an argument with our staff director, Marissa.

"And you're gonna take my phone privileges away for what?"

"Because you lied and hopped a bus to see your boyfriend even though he's grown and you're underage, and that's it, young lady. Now go get washed up for dinner." Marissa's tall, imposing stature made Nellie turn red. "He's nineteen! I am seventeen! We're teenagers! And how dare you when *she* keeps doing chores for her sister, and none of you call her out on it!"

April stood frozen with the dishes, Lauren idled in the kitchen behind her, and Faith and I stood at the head of the table, still holding silverware.

"Don't bring them into this; they've barely been here for two weeks!" the college intern, Anna, chimed in.

"Nah. Nah, 'cos she was just outside trying to steal my boyfriend! And she thinks she's cute 'cos she stuffs her bra? Give me a break."

Faith intervened, saying, "Leave my sister out of whatever you are going through! She tried being nice to you, and nobody here likes you anyway!"

"Faith, please stay out of it," I start, but Nellie is already in my face, with tearful freckles and emblazoned eyes; I see her fake an exit and then turn to swing on me.

I quickly blocked her arm and struck her on the right side of her face.

She slams me into the grandfather clock, and I push her into the doorways. April and Lauren have scurried off somewhere; Marissa is yelling that she's going to call the police, and Annie and other staff intervene, too. But I go into a barrage of flying fists into this girl's face, chest, arms, whatever I can see in the split-second melee. I realize I'm winning and start to back off, but Faith leaps in and jumps on the girl's back, screaming in a rage.

After the commotion settled, Nellie and Faith were punished. Nellie's day passes, phone privileges, and job duties were all revoked, and her only allowance was her schoolwork and an after-school job she could keep with verified sign-in and sign-out sheets.

Faith was later sent to a P.A.L. Mission in Canton.

"We have noticed that you don't do your chores, Faith, and that is a stipulation of your being allowed to stay here. We've also heard times when Jordan would try to talk to you, and you would attack her, but she kept covering for you. Well, we can't accept this behavior, Faith."

And that was the last word on it.

Faith was moved one day when we had all left to go to the grocery store, and after we had unloaded everything, all that was left in our room was the dry-erase board Faith had written "Faith and Jordan's place" on.

I felt hollow and empty still without my feisty other half being there. However, I decided to remain hopeful that we'd still get to see each other if we followed the rules.

Life at PAL picked up; I got my first job at a baby's clothing store called Bearly Worn and had adjusted to making new meals each week with Lauren and April.

We had even sort of become a little clique, walking together arm in arm at the end of the summer festival, Lauren saying, "They're gonna love you at our high school. They would've loved you and Faith together especially. Like sista-sista!" She sang out jokingly, referencing the twin sister TV show, and we all laughed reminiscently at the idea.

Faith at Odds, in P. A. L Mission Canton, Ohio

As we were coming home, taking off our party beads, April called out, "Jordan! Phone's for you!" And I dashed over, anxiously waiting to hear how my sister was.

"Faithy!" I exclaimed, so happy she was in one piece. Even if she was feisty and ornery, I knew deep down, as she always said, "I'd die if it was just me here," even though she'd never show that side of herself too often. "Oh, I'm so happy to hear from you. Thank God you're all right! We just came back home from the festival. How are you?"

"No, I'm not all right, okay! Wooo, yay, yeah, you're just having the time of your life while I'm stuck here with these desperate, jealous, lame chicks!"

"No, I miss you! I never wanted you to leave; you just would never listen to staff rules!"

"And you did? Stealing Amanda Bynes' clothes from Steve and Barry's til they searched my room. You did chores, so you're a saint? They don't care about you, so please stop thinking they do. Still acting like Asia!"

CHAPTER 17:

Flashback to Wooster Blues

Faith was right to criticize my thievery, a bad habit I had been talked into by our old childhood friend from Wooster, Asia. Asia and Shayna lived next door to us after we had left the Battered Women's Shelter. John had given up the search looking for us, and Faith and I went to sixth and seventh grade in public school for the first time in years. Our mom now had to work full-time to keep the bills paid and couldn't homeschool us anymore.

Asia's mom, Tina, was known around town to be a recovering and relapsing heroin addict, yet high functioning in the sense that she didn't look like a walking corpse like longtime hard drug users do.

She was beautiful, and so was Asia, with her olive skin, thick dark hair, and shapely figure, and Shayna, with her mom's blonde waves and porcelain features. We bonded over being raised by single mothers, even if two doors down, their free-spirited and rugged sorority-like home paled in comparison to our mother's strict Christian home, blaring gospel music on cleaning days, complete with our new little fox terrier boy named Spike we had adopted from Amish country and all-around sense of order.

One day, Asia came bursting into our door in tears, crying that her mom Tina's boyfriend had tried to rape her and that she had packed her clothes and wouldn't go back until he was gone. My mom, seeming to be having flashbacks of her own childhood, immediately leaped into savior mode, wrapping Asia up in a dramatic embrace, and tearfully asked, "Baby, was he able to fully touch you? My God, this is horrifying, to think of you in that house alone with that drunken, raving man."

"No," Asia said in a congested voice. "I kept kicking him in his private like you told me, and eventually Shayna came home and hit him on the back, making him leave."

"Good. That man is sick! I have half a mind to call probation on that pervert," my mom said, getting that familiar rile in her voice when she was about to kick John out for the umpteenth time.

"No, please don't do that. He'll go crazy on our mom if you do," the normally quiet Shayna said behind a wave of her long golden hair.

"Okay then, babies. You can stay here with me until things cool off. I'll keep talking to Tina so she knows where you are and what's happened." She caressed them both at her sides while Faith and I stood there in shock and awe. We had seen her go overboard before, but never this much.

In private, when they had left to get more of their things, Faith said with an eye roll and disdain, "You know when we were hanging out with them a few weeks back, and we came home running and screaming? It was like a week after we had tried taking them to that white church we visited because you didn't like the Baptist church we were at. You always give up the minute a pastor says something you don't like."

"Yeah, Mommy," I chimed in, also skeptical. "They were really drawing an Ouija board on a piece of paper, putting rocks as the pieces, and saying their religion was Wiccan and to not tell you. I don't know how much of her story is true, is all we're saying. Maybe we shouldn't get into it."

Unbeknownst to my mom, Asia had already confessed to me that she wasn't "all the way a virgin" once seventh grade started, but after we saw how much the rich girls were making our lives hell, even coercing middle-class kids hoping to earn cool points by bullying us, we became friends by default on the fact that nobody liked us. Asia and I specifically.

Shayna was still in fifth grade, and Faith went to the other side of the school and wasn't in any of our classes, so it was really all about hating Asia and Jordan. The animosity mainly stemmed from the fact that we both got a lot of attention from popular boys but didn't live in an affluent area.

My mom got incensed at our skepticism, saying, "Do you think Asia would lie or brag or be happy about a grown man trying to molest her? She confided to me that she isn't a full virgin due to already being molested last year, but to not tell you two that. So please don't say anything to that poor child when she gets back. I promised her I wouldn't. Even looking at the raggedy clothes they brought over, it sickens me that all their underwear is blackened and worn, ugh, falling apart. I tried scrubbing it, but it's no use. Jesus, Tina hasn't even taught those poor girls how to properly take care of themselves. I'm throwing it out to give them some of yours that are period-stained. That little girl and I prayed together, and I let her know that she was still a virgin because it wasn't her choice to give it away. This could be a breakthrough in these girls' lives that they never would've had! Do you think when Ebert would come in the middle of the night grabbing and twisting my breasts until I cried and screamed that that made me happy? *No*, it didn't. You have no idea what it's like to be a power-less child at the hands of a monster. Thank *God* that for all my faults, nobody took your innocence from you.

"Jordan, go make a pallet on the floor for them, and Faith, go through your old clothes and see what you can spare. I don't want to hear another word of this witchcraft nonsense from either of you. Do you hear me? I said do you *hear* me?" She huffed, and under the groans of Faith at the mention of Ebert, we both said yes and darted off without another word.

Back then, my mom was keen on still spanking us since we were thirteen, still small enough to be intimidated by the bareback spankings with wooden brooms; we scurried off begrudgingly so.

"Yeah, she cares *so* much about saving some random strangers while *we* have nothing! No cellphone. No name-brand school clothes. No activities. No dad. Nothing!" Faith grumbled as she gathered some clothes we were going to donate to Goodwill.

"Yeah, I know, sissy," I said, trying to ease her tensions which I fully shared. "Maybe this will show her how much we're missing when she starts helping them," I said, trying to be encouraging.

"Ha, yeah, right," Faith said with a scoff.

"And once they see her true side... when she starts yelling and cursing at them to do chores precisely, we'll just stand there and stare. They'll be begging to go back home just watch."

This grim yet predictable foreshadowing brought a wry smile to Faith and seemed to lift her spirits at what would inevitably unfold. "Exactly. Can't wait for them to see what we deal with. Won't be as bad as it is for us, but for them to have to follow the rules? Have a bedtime. Wash the dishes exactly the right way, with a capful of bleach," Faith said, prodding.

I chimed in, "Folding the towels in a perfect tight rectangle to save space."

"Her favorite line: '*No*, ignoramus, not like that; do it again!'" Faith said, which sent me a chill of irritation at the recollection.

"She wouldn't have the gall to spank them. Or throw a heavy house phone at their head for not cleaning the baseboards right. But still, I can't wait to see them come crying to us about how mean she is," I chimed in, reaffirming our mission to teach them through harsh experiences like we were.

"I know, right?" Faith's wry smile returned. "Can't wait."

CHAPTER 18:

Flashing Back to P.A.L. Mission

"You okay, Jordan?" P.A.L. Mission girl April asks.

"Y-yeah, I'm fine!" I stammer. "Faith, I've been missing you so much, and you waste the little time we have complaining."

"I'm not complaining! I'm here with racist chicks saying they're gonna jump me, and you don't care! Forget it and enjoy your perfect life!"

And the call ends.

It sent me into a tizzy. Not only was my twin gone and out of my care, but she felt like I wasn't there for her, and the anxiety was overwhelming.

The following weeks turned into my first month without Faith, but saw me get a phone call from her which ended with us praying together and having our normal sisterly talks in spite of our own new hardships. Our new talks consisted of spiritual supernatural gifts that only Faith and I understood. Our deep theological lessons from Marmee and our church families were all pouring through. And we felt like we had a chance at life after the fact.

I brought up the fact that foster care kids can still get benefits, but I also warned her sternly to remember that she's not in P.A.L. Mission in New Philadelphia anymore, so I don't know if all of those benefits are going to still be there but maybe if we both comply.

Faith paused and said, "True. Well, I'm still holding onto my virginity, even though I just met this fine, handsome, dark-skinned boy named Michael, who everyone was putting us together like instantly, haha," and brought up her roommates, Tamika and Margaret. "I showed them pictures of you; this one gothic girl even said you were sexier than me."

"Eew," I retorted.

But Faith interrupted, "Ugh, I know. I put her in her place. But things will be okay for us lil' bohemian. Okay, be strong, and don't get all weak and sensitive like you usually are. Okay, love you. Gotta go get my hair done. Byeee!"

Barberton, Before P.A.L. Life — Reminiscing on How Our Life Brought Us Here

Faith used to tell me that I was prettier than her because my breasts and my hips were slightly bigger than hers, but I always thought she was prettier than me, even though we were twins, it was kind of an ongoing thing, and even as we were growing up as identical twins, I noticed our differences.

Once Faith started dating Levi, she was candidly open and transparent about how she was struggling with her maturation, puberty, and a little masturbation because she wanted to be with Levi but didn't want to lose her virginity. Momma Toni sat Faith down with her on her foam mattress bed and read a book we had just picked up from a Christian bookstore in Fairlawn called Berean Bookstore. The young woman's eloquent candor helped Faith come to terms with her growing puberty.

I remember Faith would tease me for not even experimenting at the age of sixteen in Barberton.

God's way of demonstrating to me how, even as identical twins, we had our own fingerprints, minds, personalities, and, with Christ, our own individual souls. I'm grateful that my mother taught us, in spite of our Christian faith, not to feel ashamed about our maturation process as it was the natural process of life, the way God designed us.

My mom was always adamant about giving us the sex talk because she would always recollect Grandma Idella saying, "You know your granny told me how she never got that informative sex talk, and so many other girls don't either. These young baby girls go out into the world blind and are manipulated and used by disgustingly unsavory and demonic-minded people. Like the word warns us, the devil, our enemy, roams around like a ravenous lion, seeking whom he may devour. Always remember that, girls."

CHAPTER 20:

P.A.L. to Berea Children's Home

The P.A.L. Mission girls took us all to a friend's pool party the following weekend, and I made my second or third meal there. I tried to shake the uneasy feelings I had by staying busy.

Then another phone call.

"Well, now they're saying I'm being kicked out! Being sent to some place called Parmadale."

"What? What happened?" I stammered, feeling my heart sinking, trying to prepare myself for the worst.

"They said 'cause I cursed out this girl. But Jordan, she had been threatening me since day one, so I let her have it. So ugh, now we might not be able to visit each other as soon as we hoped. Don't worry, lil' bohemian," she said affectionately, a nickname for my headscarves and hoop earring phase. "I'm gonna stay strong. We're gonna make it away from these unstable people and get through it. Okay, I gotta go. Remember, fight back if you have to. I love you. I'm scared, but I'm gonna be okay. Okay, I gotta go now. Love you."

And the phone hung up.

CHAPTER 21:

The Foster Care Shuffle Before Warren

I went to my room and wailed and sobbed, truly feeling like the room was spinning. Just my magazine pics and blue comforter swirling around in my head.

I woke up to Marissa softly knocking on my door and then coming in.

"I suppose you heard the news that your sister had been sent to Parmadale. That place is for the worst of the worst kinds of kids. Violent kids. Kids with a criminal history. Kids that are honestly nothing like you or your sister. I wish we could take her back, but we just can't cater to people who won't work with the program. I hope you know that we all found it endearing that you'd do your sister's chores for her, even when she was so mean to you at times. You still have a chance here, though. The ladies at Bearly Worn love you; they tell me how polite and helpful you are. It doesn't have to end for you just because it has for your sister. You can do great things here."

Her enthusiasm and positivity almost made me want to believe it. But unbeknownst to her, my heart was sinking and breaking. My faith was gone. If only she could fathom how utterly devastating this was to me.

The next day, I felt like I had lead for legs and couldn't move. I did breakfast and routines in a lackluster daze. I waited for Lauren to go to work and April — who asked several times to hang out, but I just wasn't ready to yet — eventually left, and I was finally alone.

Even before foster care, my mental health had begun spiraling out of control; amid the screaming fights between John and Mommy, hearing glass breaking and loud cries through the walls, the divorce, and various moves were all taking its toll.

Faith's depression and despair grew as we left the comfort of our home to live with strangers and shouldered the weight of all the household chores, making sure my mother's fibromyalgia was tended to, and bearing the brunt of both my mother and sister's mental health issues that they were refusing to work with was gradually leading me into self-harm and silent devastation. Faith's consistent verbal and sometimes physical attacks on me when our mom would go to work and even occasional suicide attempts borne out of the desperation of wanting to defy my mother's insistence on homeschooling us, which was now practically impossible with her being a single mother working full time.

Faith's most notable attempt at hurting herself was during a move from a battered women's shelter in Canton before we got to Wooster. Faith suddenly lunged towards me with a butcher knife, waving it chaotically, then trying to stab herself. She rushed to an open window, yelling that she would slit her throat before I was able to wrestle the knife from her hand, and it fell into the bushes.

I would rarely, if ever, tell my mom about Faith's dramatic antics, bottling up everything, even when I needed her the most. Cutting myself became a way for me to release my anger and build self-hatred at my own helplessness, something I had stopped doing for a few years but had always been a demon of mine, plaguing me.

I took a razor and began cutting my arm.

Feeling the searing pain and pressed until it matched the soaring pain I was feeling in my heart. I sobbed and felt my body turn electric hot, almost shaking with pain. Thinking of how my mom didn't want us to be separated. Our old life in Barberton was slipping away. My beagle, Macy, had just been adopted by a family friend. And now my last link to home was gone.

"Jordan! Time to run some errands; hurry up! All the girls are back, and we're loading up the van!" came a shout upstairs, and in a panic, I attempted to disinfect, wrap, and cover it up with a long-sleeved shirt.

I clamored to the sink, washing my hands furiously, wincing, "Okay! Just a second, I'm getting dressed!"

I picked up some rubbing alcohol, thinking it was peroxide, and I poured it into the three gashes I had just put on my wrist and felt the most incredible, visceral pain shooting down my skin that I had ever felt in my life.

I screamed loudly, "Oh my God. Oh noo. Ah, God," and felt a hair's breadth of relief because, for those few seconds, I wasn't grieving Faith.

Anna was climbing the stairs and saw the droplets of blood and my arm oozing, and she immediately ran downstairs for the first aid kit.

The day was halted because of my self-harm incident, and I heard whispers of what to do with me. I grew more and more irritated at them, still harboring some misplaced sense of loyalty to my twin, even to my own detriment.

I remember Annie lovingly saying, "Nobody will make this room a home the way you girls did. All your magazine wall collages." She paused, seeming to get choked up. "I really wish you weren't hurting this much and that you didn't have to leave."

"M-maybe I don't have to leave?" I said with feigned hope. I knew it wasn't possible, but I still thought I might as well try.

"We just don't have the resources to treat self-harm and mutilation. A facility with mental health professionals on site would be able to treat these types of illnesses more efficiently than we ever could."

I never forgot her words or her sweet and mournful voice of encouragement. That she still saw me, the *real* me. Not the trauma.

And so, the road to Berea Children's Home ensued.

CHAPTER 22:

Berea Children's Home

When I finally arrived at BCH, I felt like I had stepped into a terrifying lifetime movie.

Started to think that I should've just quietly suffered at home under my mother's stifling forced homeschooling, bareback broom spankings, and verbal abuse coupled with flashes of her former suburban self was better than this.

It was too late now, and there was no going back.

"Drop your duffel bag over there. I'm Derrick, the house manager... Hey, kids! No footballs in the house! Sorry, hah. I'm the shift lead till my relief comes, that is. We're doing shift change right now, but I'll have Sara show you your room."

I was guided by a staffer to a room with two bunk beds and I plopped down on a bottom bunk, next to the sheet and thin pillow they gave me, for a long time.

Eventually, I was sitting in the dark, not ready to go into a new world that I was already in.

The friendly black gentleman who had done my intake was back. "There's dinner downstairs if you're hungry. Chicken nuggets and fries, yummy stuff. Come on."

I walked out into the hallways where green and yellow walls with paintings of trees and flowers from kid residents greeted us.

"Here's our office. Most of the time, you're only in here if you're in trouble, but you're a good girl; I can tell you won't be in here much."

I listened and clutched my arm, which was still raw and somewhat throbbing; I asked if he had any gauze.

"Gauze? Why would you need gauze? Oh, dang," he gasped, looking at the oozing arm I had unveiled.

Sara came back and wrapped my arm for me, but Derrick was on the phone in a hushed tone, muttering, "She cuts," and "We don't know what to do about self-harm. She'll have to be sent to STC. But it's the weekend. Okay, Monday. We'll see."

I didn't know what STC was, and I didn't care. I was giving up on myself and starting to hate the world and everyone. For seeking help and it being no match to help the complex situation of our home life. For my sister, being unruly and difficult. And myself, for being trapped in it.

I made fast friends with a flamboyant gay boy, Tyrell. He was fawning over my looks and the clothes I had packed; I figured he'd do.

"Ooh, girl, you have a nice grade of hair. You should let me hook you up. I'll do a sock bun on you; it'll be so cute and classy like you. Will you let me?" he asked.

The other little girls who had gathered shouted, "Yes! Yes! Let us do her makeup, and you can do her hair!"

"Don't crowd her now, y'all. She'll let you know when she's ready. Okay, everyone, get in line time for dinner!" Derrick shouted, and the kids seemed to understand and assembled in a line.

A couple of older boys came in from the basketball court, and Tyrell gave one a side eye, "That boy right there. A lost soul, child."

"Which one?" I asked.

"The tall, skinny boy. His name is Darnell or something. He always pushes up on the new girls, especially if they are cute, so girl, just watch out; that's all I gotta say."

I ate and asked for Tylenol PM to sleep; I just wanted to lay down and close my eyes and open them and make this day disappear.

The next day, as Tyrell and I were walking the track field, he gave me the lay of the land.

"Over there is the all-boys cottage. At first, I wanted to be sent there. Then I had ended up gettin' into it with this dude coming at me for no reason.

"What did you do for him to be mad, anyway?" I asked.

"Girl, nothin', like I said. He's just a gorilla silver-back. Just miserable. Anyway, the all-girls cottage is probably where they are sendin' you. It's not that bad. I like intake better 'cos it's a mix; it's less drama over here. Then that's STC. For the crazy, crazy kids."

"There's a fence with barbwire on the backyard, too. Dang, why?"

Tyrell shrugged. "I don't know. I just know you don't wanna end up there."

That evening, I browsed over some of their book selections, but my mind was racing; all I could think of was where Faith was or to do anything not to make me continually worry about where Faith was.

I started sketching and agreed to let Tyrell experiment with my hair.

"Yes, honey!" I got from Tyrell and squeals and giggles from the little girls going to grab their nail polishes.

Just then, Darnell and his friend came in bouncing their basketball, Darnell stealing it from the boy and dribbling it back and forth behind his back. The younger boy started whining, "Give it back!" while Darnell chuckled heartily.

"Dang, girl, you fine," he said to me as he dashed out of the room with the young boy chasing him.

"Girl. Pish. Be careful," Tyrell said.

The next night, at dinner, I was called into the office. "Come Monday, Jordan, you will be moved to the Secure Treatment Center. I told them about your arm. That's unsettling stuff; why would you do that?"

I felt embarrassed and ashamed, but I wasn't about to give in. "Because of my twin sister Faith. She's just… I don't know. She's breaking my heart. I just couldn't."

"It's okay, honey," Sara said and left it there.

After dinner, we all started talking about what we were going to watch.

"I'm gonna pick; I have the remote. I asked for it first," I said and found *Lion King* playing.

"Don't nobody wanna watch that soft movie," Darnell quipped, spinning the basketball while a few kids snickered.

The little nail polish girls chimed in, "No, we wanna watch whatever Jordan watches! Dummy!"

But Darnell was already out of his seat, trying to grab the remote from me, but the girls blocked him.

"Get outta here, dookie butt!" another little girl cried.

"Yeah, don't think we forget you dookie in the bed!" a little boy yelled, and the room erupted into uproarious laughter.

"Shut yo stupid self up!" he screeched, apparently growing mortified. The younger boy from earlier swiped his basketball and ran away laughing, and the laughter was contagious, so I joined in.

I was the oldest, so that was a big mistake.

"Man, shut yo big head up, ugly!" he screamed, and after that, the joke was over.

"Why don't you shut up and control your bowel movements!" I shouted to more laughs, and eventually, we were face to face.

He punched me in my chest, and I stood on the couch and cracked him in his head with the remote while staff members barged in and pulled him back.

"You dead after today! Know that!" he cried as he was being tackled in a restraint.

Soon, we were both pinned to the floor, screaming and crying.

I managed to wriggle my right leg out of the hold and lunged it in his direction, hearing staff saying, "Stop! You cannot fight someone while they are being restrained!"

Once the fight was over, the staff sent everyone to their room except Darnell and me.

"Jordan, I'm sorry, but in the morning, you gotta go, okay? You haven't even been here a week and already this."

"He hit me first! What kind of man puts his hand on a woman? It's pathetic. Are you serious?" I roared, but it was no use.

"You lucky you goin' there. Because it ain't over," Darnell said while holding an ice pack to his head.

Sadly, for me, he was all too right about that premonition.

CHAPTER 23:

The Secure Treatment Center of BCH

And so, the journey to the STC ensued.

On the first day in STC, I wore a Scully cap, dark corduroy jeans, and a black neutral shirt. I had started to feel like I was becoming hardened by my various foster home stints with Faith before we landed at P.A.L. Mission. I was guided into the common room/living room area after my bags were brought in and was briefed on the rules by Miss Cynthia on how the facility ran and introduced to the residents in a roll call like fashion.

Bryant, a dark-skinned boy who had glasses and a noticeable speech impediment, came up to introduce himself sheepishly.

Next was Chase, and she sat in the center of the room, telling me she was the house mother of the pod, saying that she runs everything and all the kids. She then snapped and motioned for Bryant to come back over; he grinned eerily and knowingly, rolling up his sleeve to show me his self-inflicted scars of Chase's name, done in eraser mark burns. This was a fear-mongering tactic I knew she was using to show me that he was in solidarity with her. Chase was a hefty girl and had these flared thick nostrils puffed out in pride at me as she started to walk around the common area pod to signify her dominance.

Suddenly, there was another little girl named Talia, who was about ten or eleven, explaining that she was there because her father was "touching her" in their small trailer park community.

That same day, Chase braggingly let it be known that she was having a statutory affair, or in her words, "screwing that cowboy blondie over there." She pointed to one of the staff members, a blonde guy sitting across the room eating at the desk.

"He's yummy," I lied to her, acting compliant, although I already knew that she and I would not get along. Her slight homosexual passes at me were already making my skin crawl. I resorted to allowing them to presume I was scared and sheltered and would go along with whatever they said.

The staff member, Chad, was idling by as she finished her introductions, kind of giving her a knowing smirk and looking me up and down. He then came over and introduced himself as Chad, and I asked, "How long have you been working here?" He immediately went to sit next to me extremely closely as I moved over to a separate seat.

"Sorry, I'm just shy," I said doing my best to contain my annoyance at the immediate entitled attitude of them both. I was a virgin at seventeen and determined to stay that way for Christ, Faith and I both, in spite of our family issues.

He nervously answered, "I've been here for about three or four months. My girlfriend and I just broke up, haha." He laughed somewhat nervously. "She says I work too much. I just love kids; is that so bad?" he asked in a wobbly tone, and I was immediately annoyed at him for being unprofessional and talking about his personal life when he was supposed to be a staff member and leader. Thankfully, he didn't really understand my emotion, and misreading my irritation as playing hard-to-get, he decided to try to bring me out of my shell and said, "Hey, you and Chase come out onto the patio; we're gonna go outside and get to know each other."

The other kids started to groan, saying, "Aww, we all want to go outside, too! Why can't we? Why do they get to go?"

And he said curtly, "Because she's a new girl, and Chase wants to go, and that's just how it is going to go." He was opening the secure treatment door to the outside fenced-in area with the electronic keys, and Chase and I were sitting outside by the wooden tables.

I kind of kicked the deflated basketball, looking at the basketball court and the grass dejectedly and then just the fence. "Yeah, lotta girls hop the fence," Chase said, breaking the silence after whispering with Chad. "Me and Bryant had hopped the fence a couple of years ago."

I winced at thinking of being here longer than the mandatory three months.

Chase continued, "We had hooked up, but we got caught like two weeks later," with low chuckles and coughs.

Chad cut in, surprised, saying, "Oh, you hooked up with Bryant?"

She hurriedly said, "Oh, no, no, no, not really, honey, we only had time to take a shower, then we got caught." I rolled my eyes and ascertained how she rested on her bullying tactics for survival.

Later on in the night, as we were winding down, Chad came and tapped on my door as I was reading a letter from my sister. He stood for a moment, asking me what I was doing, and before waiting for an answer, he sat on the edge of my bed, telling me, "You know you're beautiful. Not like Chase, hah. She keeps me centered. But you? You're different. You seem more mature than your age."

I was newly seventeen and nodded as I was silently thinking, *This is not about to be a lifetime movie where I get molested because this guy is still a kid in his mind. I guess he thinks I've never had any home training and want some attention or validation so much that I'll take it.*

I pretended to comply with him when he said that the next night he was going to visit me at eleven o'clock because the staff wouldn't be there, and it would just be him on duty.

The next morning, I told Mr. Adam in secrecy; we were getting our medications handed to us one by one, and I passed him a post-it note about Chad's creepy bedroom visit and allowing only Chase and I out without supervising the other kids, which could be found on film. I passed it to him as I was getting my anti-depressant Abilify medicine and then went about the day with everyone else, with nobody being the wiser. I was later called into the office, where I relayed the incident and his unprofessionalism, Chase's bragging, and bluffed it as a new girl protocol to suspicious residents. Two weeks later, I noticed Chad hadn't been back since that day.

I saw him sitting in his car through the window in the hallway there, and he was crying, looking down and wouldn't look up at me. I just stared at him for a long time because I guess he was transferred to the all-boys cottage, and later, he resigned.

Chase was immediately enraged at my exposing her, even though I only did it to safeguard my own virginity because I was still in the mindset of living for Christ and denying my flesh. Reading memory Bible verses with my mother when she would come home from work at her real collecting office job share secured in Barberton.

I knew Chase wasn't having it; she recruited another girl named Jaquita, who was very loud and brash and sassy, and even at fifteen, already had the shape of a grown woman, swarthy skin, tiny little ponytail that she always wore, and noticeable halitosis. Jaquita's breath had become a running joke about how offensive her breath was to people. A new boy resident, George, called her out on it when she walked up to him shouting, "Why you act too good to write a note back just cause somebody liked you, now you think you are somebody!"

George replied, "Yeah, anything to get away from your rancid breath!"

And Jaquita hauled off and punched him, making his head bobble, immediately sending all of us kids into our rooms for lockdown.

Chase had initiated Jaquita to start honing in on me during my first week at STC and to basically attack me at random, still incensed about me getting Chad fired. One afternoon, I was going to put away my art supplies because I had begun furiously sketching and documenting the time there, thinking of taking the time to make it a book, but mainly to keep my sanity as my world felt like it was spinning out of my control.

Anyways, this hater girl Jaquita, as I have my back turned, throws a hard cup towards my room as I'm putting my things in my pencil case, I whip my body around to try and face her behind the idling staff member Brock, trying to block my path.

She's continuously yelling at me from her bedroom door, shouting, "New chick! New chick! Get out here and finish what you started! I don't know who you think you are cause you nobody! Nobody cares about you; I don't care!" Staffer Brock, somewhat idling between us, and I start walking around him when the staffer yells at me to go to my room. I ignore him, knowing running and hiding will not stop someone who's out to get you.

I started screaming, "Who are you? What are you talking about anyway? I don't even know you!"

At that moment, she swung at me, but I instantly moved away from her swings, standing behind the staffer and the wooden couch with the loose cushions on them. From there, she kept swinging at me, edging closer and blocking my jabs. I maneuvered and dodged her blows, edging her closer to her door room, propped it open, and reached around the staffer, hitting my fist sideways like my stepdad John showed me, hitting the door but feeling my fist hit her shoulder with the impact. I felt a huge shove push me forward into the doorway where she was standing because she was still idling in front of her door, and she started trying to shove me into the door, but from there, the staff was already convening behind me to restrain us. The staffer boy darted around Mrs. Cynthia, holding me, and tripped her on her face in a swift restraint. The staffer, Brock, threw her over on her stomach as I was thrown on my stomach.

I was almost on top of her, and I was still trying to reach for her. She and I were still grasping at each other, and she attempted a throw and almost hit me, which immediately made me angry, so I threw a right kick that actually connected to her foot. Mr. Adam began screaming, "You can't hit somebody who's being pinned down! That's a cowardly move!"

I was like screaming belligerently, "Yeah, you be in here, then." From there, I dedicated the rest of the month to model behavior, a turnaround maneuver that I knew would rattle my opposition. They're so used to fast-paced public school and street life; I knew that patience was my biggest asset in overcoming the hazing.

My head was on fire, my eyes were rolling back in my head, and I had a growling voice. It was a growl because of the relentless feeling of wanting to survive and all the time I was losing being here. Faith and I had stifled angst built up over years of traumatic family issues, and those emotions were all erupting at this time. At seventeen.

CHAPTER 24:

Separated Sisters Trying to Process Foster Care

My Diary Entry — August 15th, 2008

Dear diary.

Yes, thank You, Jesus, for answering my prayer. Finally, my sister called me last night, and it was so nice to hear her voice. For the most part, our conversation went better than our visit with Mommy.

"Hello, hello, Faith?"

"Yeah, Jordan?" Faith answers anxiously, and I hear kids giggling in the background.

"Hey, Faith! Wow, what are you doing?

"Nothing right now. So, are you getting along with the kids there?" Faith asks pointedly, back in her mothering tone of voice.

"Yeah, I guess. I mean, the kids are okay. I just don't get all buddy-buddy with them."

"But seriously, don't try to, though. Okay?"

"Yeah, I know. I've already been doing that since I got here; these kids are crazy."

Faith sighed. "Yeah, I know they are. I really miss you. I was crying today. I miss you too all the time; it's weird not seeing you."

"Why were you crying?" I asked, stunned she still cared.

"Because I was lonely, and I just was sad because I missed you. You were sad, too?"

"Yeah, I was sad all day. Then some of the kids started saying that I talk white, of course. So, I almost got in a fight with someone, but I stopped before I got in trouble. Are the kids doing that to you, too?"

"No, they're just doing stupid gossip stuff and talking about me and stuff like that."

"Yeah, they're doing that to me, too," I replied assuredly. "Same old, same old. Annoying ghetto people. But anyways, aren't we supposed to see each other with our caseworker, or are we doing that next week?"

"She said we can see each other on Monday, Tuesday, and Thursday next week."

"All those days?" I said, trying to stretch our conversation. Our phone calls were now our only sisterly time.

"No, just one of those days out of the week, silly. So, what are you doing after this?" Faith asked, her twinly sisterly vibe coming back.

"Sitting around, then we have to go to bed soon," I say, tracing the phone line.

"Yeah, me too. Hey, they're rushing me off now. I love you," Faith says behind some muffled background voices.

Before hanging up, I say, "Love you, too. Say your prayers tonight."

"I will, lil' bohemian. Say your prayers, too. Talk to you later. Love ya. Okay, bye."

That's all I can remember from our conversation, minus some things I left out. Now, the kids in here are all against me because of me getting Chad fired.

They all like to mess with this little kid, Jovan, because they know he'll react negatively and get in trouble. They also whisper things like "fatty" to him when he walks by and then pretend like they didn't say anything and laugh at him when he gets in trouble for overreacting to their taunts.

I decided to speak up about it once it happened during our pH group therapy sessions. I said it vaguely, "I mean, I'm not mentioning any names, but I see people whisper stuff to him so he can get in trouble —"

In mid-sentence, I was cut off with a, "No, we didn't, you don't even know what you're talking about!" from Jasmine.

"You're lying. You just like to get people in trouble," from Chase.

And, "You're a liar," from Delicia.

I replied calmly, saying, "I'm not a liar; I just see you guys making fun of him and talking about him."

"And we talk about you too! So now!" Jasmine retorted.

Delicia added, "Yeah, and you need to get points taken for MYOB — mind your own business — so be quiet."

Brian interjected, making a fake cough thing, saying, "Uhhuhh. I'm allergic to bull crap" in his weird half-asleep, half-awake voice, his eyeballs always wandering all around. He has a lazy eye that roams, especially when he's making fun of somebody, which makes him all the more unattractive.

They've all been talking about me, but I can honestly say that I don't care. I will still be courteous to them, but I couldn't really care less about them. They're monstrously unintelligent, uncouth, and have no future. It's obvious that's all they'll be, so I refuse to give in. I won't. I have too much to live for. Now we're in our second pH, and we just got done meditating. You have to have a word to do it properly. My word was calm. Once I said it in my head, I heard other voices chanting it with me and felt better. I have to go. I'll talk to you later.

August 23rd, 2008

Hi, diary.

It's been a little while. I went on a clothing voucher yesterday and got some really cute skinny jeans and different colored collared shirts with some frills on them for school. It's harder to shop for clothes now with getting curvier. I'm gonna rip an exercise article out of Shannon's magazine when she gets back; gonna keep it on the DL for now, lol.

When I got back from my clothing order, Jovon was in another restraint in the living room, so we were locked in the hallway. Bryant was sitting in front of the closet where our personal boxes were.

I saw my sister a day ago, and she looked so pretty and different. More mature. I had forgotten what she looked like, but I was so happy to see her. At first, I was mad and frustrated because, like, already getting "stepped down," which means she gets to move into a house with fewer rules and more leniency. With cable, cozier bedrooms, your own jewelry, and comforters. I was upset about that and the fact that she noticed that I gained some weight. She's 125 pounds now, but she used to be 115. I used to be 118, and now I'm 128, probably 130 now. I can still wear three and five in jeans, but because I already have that tone from working out before here.

I eventually got out of my funk even though I kept obsessing over how bad I looked in the digital camera when our caseworker took pictures of us. I'm going to track down Mr. Jeff, the head director here, and basically beg him politely to go to ML, which is more relaxed and comfortable.

I got a note from my mom, and everything seems to be working out for her. Nana has helped pay off some of her old debts, and she's enrolled back into school. Ali has also gone back to school and is getting straight As.

August 27th, 2008

Yesterday was a disaster. I got into two restraints because I got sick and tired of people talking about me and muttering rude comments in the midst of my struggle. Chase, Jasmine, Delicia, and even Denise all mocked my cries and left. My worst nightmare happened and is happening now. I exploded at them to say it to my face and for the staff to do something about it.

Mr. Nick came in, saying, "Yeah, now I can see why you're here," like the jerk that he is.

I decided to write my mom a really long note and try to get out what we can never get out in person and see what she says. Either way, to start over and forgive her. At least, if I do go home, I'd have a little less stress. I'm gonna try to call Faith and talk to her about it. It feels weak for me to be giving in, but I just have a lot of mixed feelings right now. I know she just got out of the hospital for high blood pressure, and I feel guilty. Like I should be there for her, but also like she should be *there for me. I wrote a copy of the letter that I sent my mom, hoping to see what she says.*

"Dear Mommy. I know we don't ever get to talk through the circumstances to write you this, and you need to know all the reasons behind everything that has happened. I just want to let you know that before I start this, this isn't an 'I hate you, you're a horrible mother' letter at all.

"I'm just explaining how I feel to you. I love you very much; you'll always be my mom, no matter what. Well, the reason this all started was because I was torturously miserable and despondent, and my body was subconsciously expressing it.

"Every day on 6th St. in Lake Anna was the same. Force myself to get up, get dressed for no reason, walk the dogs and force my brain to teach itself history, algebra, and more. On top of that also motivate and encourage you to get out of bed, followed by massages, constant pep talks, making your lunch, and also having to make sure the house was in tip-top shape, often without Faith's help. I had no friends. I had absolutely nothing to do all day. Walking into places and having people stare because they didn't know me and wondered why I wasn't in school. But I masked all that so I wouldn't upset you. With all your bills, constant car worries, repossession repair, etc. Along with the constant support I'd have to give you about your job issues, friends, and boss troubles, I could have never told you even the slightest thing without overburdening you.

"When I got fed up enough and did bring things up to you, you either blow up, call me ungrateful and spoiled, or tell me all the financial reasons you couldn't do this or that. In short, I felt pathetic. What normal teenager is so wrapped up in her mother's affairs? I could never tell you this, but I felt pathetic for looking forward to going to McDonald's or occasionally the Corral with my mom for the weekend. Being homeschooled,

which was now just you buying books from Barnes and Noble and having us learn them because you were too busy to really teach us anymore.

"And you never knew it, but Faith would start fights with me all the time, and she would destroy stuff and scream throughout the night, sometimes trying to kill herself; then, I would comfort her, and sometimes we would just have screaming matches anything we could do just not to take our lives. Whenever I thought about or attempted suicide, the only reason I couldn't go through with it was because I knew how emotionally and physically you were dependent on me. Well, days and days turned into months and years spent with these pent-up feelings. All of this didn't come out of nowhere; this was followed by escaping that hellish year in Wooster. On top of me being tortured every day at that racist school, I'd come home to your abusiveness. What I do give you credit for is that we stopped shortly after we turned fourteen, you cursing us, beating us, and forcing everything to be your way. That day when I blew up was because I couldn't take it anymore. I know you have your version, and I have mine, but seeing as I don't hallucinate, I remember what I did that day. I just went along with your story so I could go home. When I finally stopped forcing myself to tell your story, you decided to take me back to the hospital.

"Before I get into that, I want to explain what happened that night. I was in the kitchen on a Friday night, alone yet again and mad because of it, being a teenager with no social life. You came home from work with groceries on a freezing winter night, and luckily, I managed to wash the few dishes in the sink after putting them off all day before that started another riot. Anyways, you started chastising me for putting the dish drainer a little on the edge, which I thought was about to turn into an hour lecture. Yes, I know it's an issue, I guess, but I'm a teenager and human, so it's not that big of a deal. You moved it even though I wanted to and kept pushing it so far that the dishes on top would fall over. I'm not saying you did it purposely. So, I made a little remark saying, 'Oh, you messed it up,' and went to pick it up.

"This is when you exploded, saying I was a disrespectful brat over and over and that I could get all the groceries by myself. This irritated me because you were blowing it way out of proportion and punishing me. So, I ran upstairs, annoyed, and got my coat. I ran back downstairs to get it over with, and then you said, 'Just for that, I'm not getting a present for you that I couldn't even afford to buy,' along with making me drag the snow-filled trash cans by myself. I exclaimed, "Oh my God," and walked out at this point, very mad to do all this.

"When I came in, you called Faith downstairs to show her the present and the one that was mine that you were giving her. I had to go to the bathroom, but you said, 'I don't care.' And you began showing the clothes while saying, 'Look at every detail, Jordan.'

"'I have to go to the bathroom, so I guess you're gonna make me pee on the floor like a dog,' I said.

"And you replied, 'Yeah, you can. Fine! Go upstairs, and when you're done, you can get the broomstick and wait at my bed.' I knew what that meant.

"Yes, I agree my comment was rude and disrespectful and, at the most, would merit some extra chore or whatever, but a spanking? At my age, and especially the way you do them is degrading and abusive, considering all this stuff. I had enough, so I blew up, saying you weren't touching me. I ran to the attic and held a broom for protection. Yelling any horrible thing I could think of while throwing some notebooks at you.

That's when you threatened and then called the cops. I couldn't believe you were going to have me arrested when all you had to do was leave me up there and then punish me later in a different way. So, enraged, I ran into the living room to get ready to fight my point to the cops. You were already down there at this point with the phone, so you proceeded to grab me, push me, and sit on me on the couch until the cops came back because I guess you thought I was gonna run away.

"This is exactly what I did. I pushed your back because you were hurting me, then pushed your arm and shoved my weight out from under you; then, I was arrested and sent to juvie. I don't wanna argue with you about it because it's over and done with, and I just wanted you to know why I acted the way I did. You may think I'm exaggerating the isolation thing because, after months of us nagging about our anguish, you had a party for us, which was your idea, but that I never heard the end of about what demonic brats we were after the fact. You also guilt-tripped us about the fact that it was your water bill money that you spent on it. It went okay, but the house was full of strangers, excluding Chastity, Candace, and Sonia; luckily, it worked out. That's the past, unfortunately. I think this all happened for a reason. If I go back home now, it'll just be the same thing, plus babysitting Allie's kids again and with no pay, even though I love those babies.

"I'd never be able to get a job taking care of Spike, you, Melody, and Allie's other kids. I'd never be able to trudge through all those thick, in-depth books teaching myself. I'd never be independent. I love you still very much and I forgive you as well. I'm going to start praying for you every day because I want the best for you. God made Allie and the babies come back into your life so you guys can help each other. You have your mom and Patty in the church there who love you and support you, too. I think in order to heal from all that's happened, we need to wake up every day and decide to forgive and forget. We can set up visits now that enough time has passed, so you don't have to worry. I realize I still need you and always will, no matter how old I get. As far as me settling in, I'm asking if you could please bag up my clothes and other belongings in my room, like small baskets and CDs for Faith and me. We'd like the radio, if you don't mind sparing it, and a few of our headphones, too. And just call Joy when you have everything together. I don't hate you, and I'm looking forward to mending our relationship.

"Love, Jordan."

August 28th, 2008

Today is a better day, much better.

As far as the girls here, I'm still ignoring them and acting like I don't hear them. Every time they crack a joke or mutter an insult, there's not even the slightest acknowledgment from me. I can hear the frustrated silence from them. Part of what helped lessen the gossip was that I apologized to everyone. I said I was sorry to Chase for ripping up her artwork on her door. It was during positives at the end of the day when we give ourselves the group or someone in the Group A positive compliment for something good we or they did.

"I give myself a positive for bouncing back from my little episode yesterday, and I give the Group A positive for, um, just letting it not affect them and bouncing back too." I added, "Chase, I want to apologize for ripping up your pictures because they were really pretty, and I wouldn't want someone to do that to me. You can rip up something of mine if you want."

"No, no. I'm good," Chase replied, looking surprised.

I apologized to Jasmine, too, because I did the same to her. "It was immature and really mean, and I'm sorry. Your dresses were really pretty, too."

She looked me up and down and said, "Uh-huh, yeah. It's okay."

She was probably less warm because we were about to get into a fight that day because I was calling her and all her friends for always gossiping.

"I'm tired of ignoring it! Do something about it!" I said to Mr. Nick, the heavyset wannabe rapper, and he replied, "Man, I can't be here to babysit your feelings every time something happens. What do you want me to do, write somebody up every time they look at you?"

"No, I want you to do something when they blatantly do it! Tell them you're gonna take their points away, they'll lose their day, something."

It felt good to get the guilt off. That's the first and the last apology that I'm making. I'm not going back. I'm gonna stick to my plan. Hopefully, I can get my passes, which are time slots where you can go out in the real world and get back on MySpace! I know I have so much stuff waiting for me. Well, I'll talk to you later. I'm gonna go sketch some more.

CHAPTER 25:

The STC Sting

One night at STC, the kids wanted to organize a "sting" against the staff, and this time, I participated because I was already incensed at being denied my phone calls to my sister Faith. Much to my own detriment, I'd come to later find out, but anyway, it started with Tara's incident.

We found out that Tara was there for severe molestation by her own father. So much so that she had procured permanent damage from being vaginally and anally raped continuously from as young as five years old. As a horrifying result of the vile treatment she suffered, she had anal fissures or lacerations and tears in her private areas. Randomly, in her temper tantrums, she would tear and spray her reopened wounds, wiping blood all over the walls. So much in fact that she could write her whole name in it on the girls' bathroom walls. Thus deeming her with the derogatory term "bloody Mary" Tara.

At first, I befriended her out of pity and tried to coddle and guide her along the way, with her grammar particularly. She had severe tremors from her abuse that showed in her hands. She wasn't able to write legibly when she wanted to write letters to her family.

I remember her coming up to me one night when I was sitting on the couch drawing in writing and asking me, "You have such pretty handwriting; can you please help me?" I was immediately excited because I didn't even think that my little skill meant anything, but to someone else, it meant a lot.

So, I would write her out alphabets that she could trace and hopefully practice, but her handwriting was forever shaky and almost illegible.

Unfortunately, Tara was becoming a liability in the other kids' minds. Like Cara, a new biracial twelve-year-old girl who had already started dating Bryant within her first week there.

She'd sit in the common area with Talia, already lamenting, "Uhgh, men are all the same, just like my mom said."

I was just looking at her like, "Little girl, please," as if she had really experienced enough life to be a pessimist.

As we were taking our turns for showers for bed, I remember Cara rushing, coming out of the bathroom, screaming, "Oh my God! Get this crazy chick out of here, man!" and staff ladies ran in. I ran behind them, and I saw why in horror.

The bathroom wall across from the shower had big, thick, bloody words saying "Tara," dripping down heavily onto the floor.

The staffer Sara muttered, "My God. I think she mixed it with soap to create the like, ugh, foaming look to it. We have to call the doctor," and they were off.

"Don't try to defend her, Jordan. She's getting outta here, for real now, nasty self."

Denise, Cara, Bryant, George, Talia, and even quiet Shannon were creating a crowd circle around Tara and me.

"*Ugh.* Look!" Bryant shrieked, almost poking at the paper clip she had screwed in so deep into her wrist that we couldn't even see it underneath her flesh. Only the greenish-grey outline poking through her arm.

"Stop! Eew, don't touch it!" Chase shouted, eyeing me up and down as she knew the kids were turning their attention away from me.

She would immediately be sent to Belmont Pines, a psychiatric hospital a few hours away, and whispered to me, "It's okay! I'll get ice cream and stuffed animals at the hospital, haha!"

"But don't you know it's gonna just make you have to stay longer, right?" I retort, shocked at her cavalier attitude.

"Oh, well. At least I get to get outta here!" She laughed eerily and was put on a hospital stretcher and carted off into an ambulance.

During that time, Bryant used her acting out to start throwing things at the walls and the new boy. George started doing the same thing. Only he was sadistically carving out bloody swastikas into his skin because he was German and screaming that he was going to murder his father once he got out of there, and other kids started cutting themselves to overwhelm the staff. Staff ran to convene in their office to call other staff members for help, and I remember, in my own sorrow, being a follower for once instead of a leader, just to see if it was worth it. If I'd get loyalty from them, against my better judgment, heartbroken for Tara's young despair.

I said, "Oh, well, God. Give us a reason," to myself, then indulged in the eraser burn self-harm sting of the day and later was sent to Belmont Pines myself.

What I didn't know is that the MP3 player I had got for Christmas, that I even coerced a staff member to load music on for me, was stolen by this new girl named Keira during the hysteria.

Kiera, aka Miss Wrecker, as she called herself, was only fourteen but was already accustomed to having a pimp, much to everyone's concealed shock.

When she arrived a week prior, she was talking about how much she missed making love to her "daddy" in their apartment and smoking blunts and drinking liquor with him. Anyway, we bonded about talking about our sisters, and she told me she thought I was smart and able to really hustle some bucks together out and about. The prospect sounded so exciting, but her sister had already aged out and had her own apartment while mine was still in my shoes, so I told her this. And that I was still a virgin at seventeen.

She squealed, saying, "Dang, girl, in my neighborhood, that wouldn't last long, just sayin'. I'm bouta be outta here, though, girl. You can still come if you want."

I silently fantasized about us being top models in downtown Cleveland, but to really think of myself at seventeen, even two years older than her, really doing that was unimaginable.

During the sting, Kiera, seemingly disappointed in my participation and using the distraction for her own escape, went into my pencil case and stole my MP3 player before she AWOLed to go be with her pimp.

My heart fell when I went for it after I got back a week later, and it was gone. I decided not to beat myself up for it, though, being understanding to myself. Taking it as Kiera's streetwise and hard lesson about being a follower when you're born to be a leader.

After my shock, I realized I still had my arts and crafts, my pencils, and my notebooks, and I realized that even without my music, I could survive and be thankful for what I still had.

I was gifted at art from a young age, and it really made me think about how valuable pen and paper were because it's something that an educated mind wouldn't want to steal, but it's also something that you can have with you forever and will withstand the test of time. Some little electronic piece needs to be charged and will just die. A page's words will never die unless you crumple it up; those words will live on forever because they're from your heart.

At STC, there was a white boy resident who had the same name as me, Jordan. The staff jokingly asked, "And say, what are we gonna call you?"

I said, "Just call me Jordan, the girl one. I dunno," sarcastically.

They eventually decided to call me Jordan Eff and call him Jordan Bee. Jordan Bee was dating teenaged Shannon, who always wore fuzzy bunny slippers, had brown, shoulder-length hair, and a sweet, soft voice.

But it was Denise the one that really influenced my stay at STC.

On our day passes, when we would go and have shopping trips or privileges for good behavior, I would start being in my klepto ways again, a bad habit I had gotten from Asia back in Wooster born out of deprivation, and swiping things and showing Denise how it was done. Only that one time she ended up betraying me and telling staff, and all the kids that were getting things from me were obviously enraged, and it actually shifted the crowd from attacking me because the kids were starting to make my life hell after Chase coerced them to start attacking me, and that was my boy to gain their attention and support, but showing them that my actions were genuine and that I could back up my promises with the results.

Denise had explained to me how she was a twin sister too, and when I told her about my twin and how I was worried about her, she would stare at me in far away disbelief or confusion, like she couldn't relate, which was weird to me. People told me that she was a pathological liar due to years of being locked in her mother's apartment as a forced sex prostitute because her mother was a severe drug addict, and from age as early as five or six, she told me.

I remember her having very ragged temple skin, a small little nose, scraggly hair, and yellow teeth. She seemed to have lived way longer than her seventeen years and looked like it as well. She also seemed to have some authority over Bryant and the other kid, Jovon, a biracial boy prone to random acts of violence and temper tantrums.

Jovon could always be heard in an ear-piercing wail during his restraints. During my own restraints, I could feel my rib cage pressing against the concrete, knowing any more pressure could cause a serious issue. I had learned how to control my breathing and slightly inch my ribs into a breathable position without having to beg staff to release me. This faint power of mental strength seemed to intimidate the staff, who had become hardened from years of dealing with violent, unloved, and unwanted children and eagerly searched my eyes for even the slightest inkling of weakness or fear. The mental strength and prayer life I had became my lifesaver during these brutal moments.

The next week, a boy named George, a white boy who wore skinny jeans and was into Lil Wayne and heavy death metal, came in and was attractive in the face, so girls were immediately finding out and running and swimming over him, and then one little girl to Leo was even making so many sexual remarks in her breath about him, which was very uncomfortable for me to think about her already being so sexually mature. Anyways, George came even though he was from a rich family suburban family; he was sent there for rebelling against his father, stealing his car as a vengeful move because of him divorcing his mother.

But later, after some time had passed, I gained privileges to go to the open cottage for good behavior, for school purposes only.

CHAPTER 26:

The Day My Faith Died, December 13, 2008

Back from Belmont Pines Psychiatric, the next day began in the same routine as usual. My world had imploded and erupted into my worst nightmare, yet the facility seemed unphased. Wake by 6 a.m., shower and dress, do some rushed chores in the common area, have a rushed breakfast of a cereal of our choice, and then onto school. I had been given the privilege to go to class in the "open cottage" for good behavior and it should be time for me to be going to school by now. I became somewhat of a model citizen, much to my embarrassment, but it was a nice respite from the toxic environment of locked up and angry kids. That would all change today.

At school, the kids from the open cottages had been briefed on my sister's death during restraint and her impending homicide trial. When I came in, one of the boys, Khris, who was a known hothead and a crude flirt, exclaimed, "See? That's why I need to be *outta* here, man! 'Cos y'all a really kill a nigga in here, man! Y'all should let her out!" he finished his rant with a cry.

"Quiet!" our teacher screeched. "Do not speak ill of the dead and especially not while Jordan is present. We all know a terrible accident has happened, and we need to work together." The word accident hit me and began stoking that unquenchable fire in my heart that hadn't gone away since I got to this place.

"It wasn't an accident! They killed her! Murdered her with their brainless brutality because they're the scum of the earth! So mad that a poor little black girl was beautiful and intelligent enough to organize kids they can't even control without force!"

"That's enough, Mrs. Finley. Any more, and we'll have to call staff in here."

Another boy screamed, "She's right!" He was a tall, light-skinned boy who was somewhat new but, at only fifteen, had a baby on the way. "They killed another boy in the juvie I was at. Devils need to die themselves."

"That's enough!" our normally composed teacher cried in a flurry of emotion. Khris got up quickly and threw a book and some papers at the teacher.

"You know none of y'all care if we live or die! Look at Jordan; she has been the only respectful one in here, and y'all killed her sister!"

Suddenly, a group of four staff members barged in with combat shields, restrained Khris, tripping him on his face and tackling him into submission while giving him a shot. He groaned and growled and stared at me with tear-filled eyes. I ran out of the classroom and was escorted back to the STC, and instead of cooperating, I went to my room and sobbed until I couldn't anymore.

CHAPTER 27:

Facing the Wake & Trial

Eventually, Faith's wake day arrived, and it was officially time to accept it… and somehow come to terms with the fact that her death was real; it was happening, and there was nothing I could do to stop it. I paced outside of the Secure Treatment Center (STC), waiting for my aunt Mara and, hopefully, my mom to take me to the funeral home. It ended up being my sassy guardian ad litem, Eliza, complete with her full face of contoured makeup and a double set of fluttery eyelashes.

"Hey, love! Time for another road trip!" she squealed jubilantly out of her red VW bug window into a puff of winter air at me, putting me at slight ease. I was happy to see it was someone comforting and not going to interrogate me to death like my relatives tended to do. Eliza had been the one who'd originally driven me from Faith and my last placement in New Philadelphia at P.A.L. Mission Girl's Group Home.

The long car ride to the Wake brought back memories of when I first met Eliza, my new guardian ad litem, and the impact that her counsel had on me. On our way out of Berea Children's Home toward Faith's wake took my thoughts back to our intimate car ride conversation that we had on our first ride up to BCH just over a year prior to this day.

Drive to Berea with Eliza and Explaining Family Dynamic

As we were driving, Eliza sensed my uneasiness and offered to play the radio. Brandy's "Right Here" song, soulful and warbly, came reverberating out of the speakers, and suddenly felt like it was all around me. The lyrics and anguish in her heartfelt vocals were pricking at my own heart or my chest. Like a pulsating pump underneath my epidermis, barely concealed. Eliza, sensing this in me, quickly switched the station from R&B to a hip-hop station. Then Lil Wayne's latest womanizing anthem, "Every Girl," came on, and the casually vulgar lyrics seemed to mock the severity of the despair this day was having on me. It's crazy how when someone you love dies, it feels like the entire world should freeze the way your heart has, but it doesn't. Only you freeze while the world continues on in slow motion around you. I guess they call this the first stage of grief, fight or flight, or whatever.

To those who know all too well the "shock of suffering," as T. D. Jakes calls it, it's a feeling that's all too visceral, all too encompassing, almost choking, and only comfort can somewhat assuage the anxiety. Something as seemingly cavalier as a hip-hop song seemed to mock this day, seemed to reduce my pride to ashes, bringing in warm and flooding tears that were burning my nostrils and face.

Eliza quickly shut off the radio, saying, "Okay, no music or radio, that's cool. We can do that." She paused for several minutes to give me time to regroup, slightly caressing my shoulder, much to my own comforting embarrassment. She suddenly broke the silence and started talking openly about why she wanted to work in foster care in the first place. She seemed to sense that I felt like her concern was more of an empty gesture than genuine.

"Most people that wanna help people have been through some jacked-up-ishhh," she said, adding emphasis to the last bit and slightly giggling at the irony of it all. "Like, I legit grew up in a household of *all* boys. It was like I was literally like their momma most of my life, yeah. Our mom dipped when we were really little and totally abandoned us to be with our completely unstable father. So, after all that, our home became a rough place to grow up for a while, 'cos my Dad never really got over my mom ditching him… but I was still like the rock for my brothers."

I was glad that Eliza decided to fill the silence because the entire thought of going to see my twin sister's dead body, as each minute passed by, the anxiety of my seventeen-year-old self was grateful for the respite of someone older, who was bravely wearing her heart on her sleeve with a fragile client. A rarity in foster care in most cases.

She continued, "Anyway, I graduated high school a year early, aced high on my ACTs for early enrollment into college. Got my bachelor's degree in psychology by the time I was twenty-one, then became a guardian ad litem to try and help kids out like me. It started out as just a part-time job to get me through college, but then I literally just fell in love with it. Getting to know the kids and creating these almost sister/brother type bonds with each other. The cool stuff we get to do all day together, the outdoor games, all of it. Which is why it's so hard for me to be taking you here."

She elaborated on how her father was an alcoholic and abusive to her and her brothers and that she escaped by becoming a mentor at school, even as early as sixth grade, and excelling at that. "That and music really saved me from my childhood…" and I nodded silently as I studied her car, the dashboard stickers of Rockstar drink labels and beads and trinkets dangling from her rear-view mirror, her elaborately long manicured nails, deep tan, and beautifully painted face. As she explained her story, I thought to myself how I could see myself hopefully becoming like her one day when I got older. But the year of me being eighteen felt like a lifetime away.

I was grateful for her opening up, briefly making me forget about my very real and immediate future. Every second, I watched the passing hilly trees; every minute, I counted the highway lines, the growing dread of what was to come. I felt like my hopes and my life were passing away at each interval. Further and further away from the dreams of Faith and I going to college together, getting out of foster care, and moving on from the drama at home, all of that now just seemed like a crumpled leaf on the highway.

Snapping back to reality again, Eliza brought me back with her matter-of-fact way of speaking; she pulled out a cigarette and paused before she lit it. "Oh, I hope you don't mind — you don't mind if I smoke a couple of hits, do you?" she said at a red light. "It's okay if you do; I'm not really supposed to, but *whew!* Hearing your story and everything… . I just hate to be taking you here…" she trailed off and got that familiar glassy-eyed look people often get after hearing about my sister's homicide case at first, which made me feel guilty for even lamenting to her, even though it's kind of her job. Doesn't matter. A homicide instantly makes you feel like it's your fault for admitting what someone took from you. A phenomenon I hope that my candor can influence others dealing with grief to discard: the notion of victim-blaming the victim and glorifying the murderer.

"No, you're fine, hah; wish I could have one too." I smiled wryly at her.

She said, "I would if I could, but I don't want you smelling like nicotine or encourage this bad habit." She groaned sharply out of the window, holding her cigarette out of the car, then got back to her point. "Listen, Jordan. From what the ladies at P.A.L. Mission told me about you and then meeting you, you're way too smart and beautiful to be going here — to this place. This place is for the worst of the worst kids. The staff ladies told me you were so responsible over there at P.A.L., doing all of Faith's chores when she wouldn't listen."

"Yeah, just like at home," I interjected. "Faith would never do chores. Faith was the track diva at home, and I was the designer sketch artist. Even though we were being stifled at home, forced to be home-schooled by our mother, who was no longer even using curriculums from the Board of Education anymore, so overprotective and controlling of us. I still wanted Faith to be a diva, though, so my mom would let Faith's domineering attitude take over, and I did, too, in a way. Even if it was at my expense… sounds dumb, I know, but a part of me felt like I owed it to her. Not to shine. So much life had been taken from us. Life that our materialistic, athletic prowess cousins couldn't wait to rub in our faces."

CHAPTER 29:

The Morgue, Wake, and Trial

I waved goodbye to Eliza and slowly walked into the funeral home. Plush pink carpet and drapery filled the room, so soft that my shoes seemed to sink into the carpet. I saw chairs and an open glistening pink casket sitting in the front room with a few people idling there, but no one I recognized from a distance. My breathing started to increase, and it dawned on me that I had never actually been to a wake before and didn't really understand what it all meant.

I ran into a man in a suit and exclaimed, "Where's my mom?"

He, looking startled, said, "Are you the other twin? My God, you look just like her. Your mother's downstairs, but wait for her up here."

I rushed away.

Down the rickety grey steps, I walked carefully as I approached a brightening light until, eventually, I realized I was in the basement. I heard my mother's voice trailing off between wails and screams I couldn't really understand. My eyes were so full of tears I couldn't see who else was in the room. I could make out a suit and a dress and my mother being held up by them, them all crowding around something.

I approached and saw that it was a table they were crowding. "No, no, it can't be her; it's not her." I gasped and nearly leaped back.

The man from upstairs came from behind, holding onto my arm said, "You don't have to do this…"

But I insisted, "No! She's my sister. It... can't be her." We walked closer, and I saw her little hands, her nails painted pink, and I turned back, saying, "No, no, I don't want to do this. No, please. No!"

But it was too late. Then I was in front of her. I gasped horribly. It didn't even look like her. It looked like her face had been peeled off and sewn onto someone's bloated, dying body. My beautiful petite Faith was now a peeling and stone shell of herself.

"Her oxygen was cut off, which is why there's so much swelling; we'll be able to get it down by the funeral..." I heard a man's voice say.

My voice broke, and I screamed as I stared at her wilting braids and her lifeless, cold hands; it wasn't my Faith! But it was. I felt my heart pounding against my chest with so much forceful pain, like it was trying to leap out of my body. I was fainting, and even with three people holding me up by both arms, I couldn't breathe.

"Please, God... tell me that's not Faith! Mommy, that's not her! My poor sister, how could they do this? Jesus... ugh, God! Please, just kill me. I can't do this, Lord... I just want to die. I can't take it..." I wailed out so forcefully that my voice shook the room as I clung to these arms for dear life.

CHAPTER 30:

Faith's Wake and Levi & Faith

Afterward, I remember that I was carried by the two people holding me from collapsing on the ground floor of the funeral home morgue. The room seemed as if it were swirling. All I could see was a grey cinderblock, bright lights, and my sister's body lying on that metal table.

Eventually, we walked back upstairs into the foyer where more distant relatives and family friends I hadn't seen in years, along with my aunt Marla and her brood, convening and dusting themselves off from the snow falling heavily outside.

We were all guided out of the main area where Faith would be prepared for viewing and for guests to say their last goodbyes to her. When we were allowed back in, a projector screen had been assembled above her glistening pink casket, and everyone was seated. I stood in the doorway, trying to imagine that the funeral was for someone else so that I may survive this day.

"It's not real. It's not Faith. It's for Granny. It's not real." I repeated this falsehood in my head several times. Maybe I could force myself and will myself into another reality. But it was impossible. The lights dimmed, and the projector started playing a reel of our baby photos my mother had collected of us: a photo of the two of us in the bathtub covered in bubbles, a picture of my mother holding both of us on a circular pillow shortly after her c-section, a picture of Faith striking one of her sassy poses as a baby, each photo like ping and dagger into my heart.

Someone asked me if I'd like to sit down, but I couldn't. I started to relent and go sit in the back row, and then a playing of a lilted version of "You Are My Sunshine" began to play over the stream of photos, and it felt like my heart would burst. Suddenly, flashing memories of my mom picking me up out of the bathtub and singing that song to us, her reading us a bedtime story from *Little Women*, and one time when we had gotten our first rollerblades and were zipping around the Hunter's Lake parking lot, and I had skinned my knee; she whispering, "You're a big girl now. That's enough crying; shake it off" while applying a band-aid. When my sniffles had slightly subdued, she grabbed me up in a warm mommy hug that only she could give me, and we rocked back and forth, humming our favorite tune until I felt better.

Then I was back here, and all of those memories felt like they had built up to this heartbreak, and I couldn't take it. I ran out of the room and went into another room, clutched the arm of a chair leg, and just started screaming. I wanted to scream the pain out of me.

It was like I finally realized the gravity of the loss I had suffered, how the memories of our life were now cut off, how I'd never get to see Faith get married, grow into a woman, graduate college, and pursue her dreams. Each thought sent my heart into a flurry. I wanted my mind to shut off, but it just wouldn't.

I remember my cousin Jalisa, along with a small group of others, staring at me from the doorway in astonishment and some with slight amusement.

Eventually, I felt a gentle hand on my shoulders that told me that it wasn't over and to please stop because I was scaring everyone. Through gasps and sobs, I walked back with her to where everyone was seated, and the video continued.

I remained at the doorway entrance. For some reason, sitting felt like I was sinking further into despair.

At that moment, I saw someone at the front door entrance coming out of the snowy rain, standing there staring at me, too. It was Levi Felding, Faith's boyfriend she had met on MySpace.

I saw Levi's tear-filled eyes staring at me in the funeral home entrance in the shadow of the unlit part of the building; his eyes were full of tears as he glanced towards the casket, then back at me. It was as if he felt the same agony as I did. Then he slowly and silently turned away; I knew his heart was shattered.

CHAPTER 31:

Meeting Faith's Roommate, Margaret, and Homicide Trial

After the wake part of Faith's funeral service was coming to a close, I remember people coming up to my mother and me and saying words.

My old babysitters, Kiana and Tiana, who had gone to high school with Allie and even accompanied us on a family road trip to Myrtle Beach, came up and said, "One day we'll go the club together when you're old enough and dance the night away, and you won't even remember all this sadness!" They said that with a forced happiness I know was hard for them to conjure up.

"And Faith will be there dancing right along with us!" Teyona chimes in.

I gave a forced chuckle as I could muster, and we hugged and said goodbye.

Then Margaret, Faith's former roommate, came up to me. "Hi, Jordan. I'm Margaret. I was your sister's roommate at Parmadale."

"Oh," I said, stunned that she was able to make it. "I'm so glad you came —"

"Don't thank me," she said with a sullen remorse that took me aback. "*None* of this should be happening. Faith was an amazing friend.

And even though those women tried to shut me up, I won't stop saying it. Faith saved my life. This girl who had it in for me since before Faith got there, for being a 'white bread' as she called it."

I winced at the cruel remark, but she, seemingly reading my thoughts, said, "Don't worry. I know your sister was nothing like that. Anyway, this girl had always threatened that she was gonna 'whoop me' for months but never did. Faith called her out on it one day, and that set this girl off. One night, when we had all gone to sleep, the girl found a metal baseball bat and came into our room. I had taken my glasses off and couldn't see who was standing over me, but as I reached for them, I heard a metal clang; then, I felt the most sharp and piercing pain I've ever felt in my life, throbbing over my head. This girl was beating me with a baseball bat to my head!" Margaret turned her head slightly to show me several stitches in her hairline that were still healing.

My face warmed with tears.

Margaret's father came behind her and put his hand on her back, telling her if it was too hard, she didn't have to, but she yanked away from him and said, "No. She needs to hear this. Faith saved my life. She literally leaped out of bed and pushed this girl off me and onto her bed; I saw her stretching her body over and laying all her weight to stop the girl from getting up while she screamed for staff. Despite all my screaming, the staff didn't come in until Faith intervened. Your sister saved my life and showed the staff up! If it hadn't been for her, the doctors said I could either be blind or in a coma. *That's* why they restrained her the next day. The kids stopped listening to the staff and were listening to Faith only. They had to make up some lame reason to restrain her so that she'd lose credibility, and they were so pissed and jealous that they killed her! If you get a chance to testify, please tell them that."

She finished her story, and it gave me a newfound confidence I didn't have before. I knew my Faith wasn't a tyrant or a monster, and now I even had a witness to prove it.

I decided that I would live, at least through the trial, to try and vindicate Faith's name.

CHAPTER 32:

Homicide Trial Ensues

The trial ensued, and I was largely not a part of it, however. I only had two visits to court to hear testimonies from the coroner, a nice and soft-spoken Indian woman who had to fight the opposing side to get the ruling of a homicide. I tried to make my eyes look as grateful to her as I could muster. When the one notably rotund woman who had once deemed herself "Faith's new mom" took the stand, her testimony sickened me to the core.

The defense attorney asked her, "You were told numerous times by the victim that you were cutting off her air supply; why didn't you stop?" And the room fell to a dead silence.

The woman's fleshy throat peered into the microphone as she nonchalantly replied, "Faith always said she wanted to be an actress. I assumed she was just acting," and my heart sank as the tears rushed out.

I ran into the hallway in a panic, not being able to breathe, and I heard whispers from some of Faith's fellow foster mates saying, "Faith? Oh my God, I thought that was Faith!"

"No, that's her twin, stupid!"

"Oh my God, she looks just like her!" I heard, and with my eyes being blurred and blinded with tears, I ran into the bathroom and sat in the stall for what felt like a long time. I heard someone enter and try my door before going to another, and I quickly dashed to the sink to wash my hands, the warm water soothing my nerves.

The person who had come in after me was approaching the sink and, in a daze, I hurriedly said, "Excuse me," and exited.

Out of the corner of my eye, I saw a large figure behind me and, to my horror, realized it was that woman. I was just polite to the woman who had caused my worst nightmare. I couldn't believe it. I resigned in my mind that this is what Christ would have wanted me to do, and I felt a sense of holy pride that I had made the Holy Spirit proud even during my own agony.

I told Mommy about it later, and she said, "Wow. I'm sorry you had to even be in the room with that wildebeest. You know. She's lucky. I really oughta tell Sean to call some of his friends from Cincinnati to take care of her."

"No, Mommy," I said, scared of this unfamiliar dark side to her I didn't recognize. "That'll only make us just as bad as her." Somehow, even the sentiment of being the "bigger person," even for a righteous reason, did little to assuage the pain that each agonizing breath we drew into this new normal.

Homicide Trial Heightens

According to a colleague, Faith was continuously writing "I want to die" on her bedroom walls; it was her way of protesting against the unfair treatment toward her friends and her, at any given moment, at the hands of staff members abusing their power in foster care.

Faith's hymen was determined as "still intact" in her autopsy. The coroner later came to find. The coroner quietly briefed us on these intimate details coming up for discussion in the anatomical report, and we thanked her mournfully. Skeletal photos depicting Faith's injuries alongside photos of her slain body were displayed. I had to leave several times, hyperventilating from the courtroom during the monotone recounting of Faith's violent murder. Details of what I was still struggling to accept determined that.

Court proceedings began after a grueling weeklong pick of jurors, I noticed that if anyone had read or knew about Faith's case and had any kind of opinion, they were not there the next week.

The defense attorney representing my mother and I began, "Where we last left off, three black women who murdered a young girl, Faith Nicole Finley, in their care. Their motive was enragement that Faith, a black girl, would defend a Jewish Margaret so vehemently, not being accustomed to a lowly foster child with such high and mighty Christian morals rivaling their own. Wanda was also the queen bee staffer who took Faith on shopping trips, and she was stung when Faith wouldn't completely claim her as her full mother." His closing defense continued with, "However, Wanda, was also not able to empathize or see Margaret as a full human being, and not another cruel oppressor in the making being lauded before her. Wanda probably viewed Margaret's illness as a convenient ploy for power through pity, which is not a part of her job description. Even Faith could see that Margaret had a real issue and needed help. She was diagnosed with diabetes so vital that she needed her insulin pump fully administered to her person to ensure that her blood sugar levels remained balanced. Which was viciously ripped from her by a so-called 'fellow white resident.' Yet, no mercy was shown. It's a miracle she survived the attack."

The prosecutor interrupted sharply, "Objection!" to which the judge sustained it, and the attorney finished.

"Faith then grabbed the metal pipe from the girl and restrained her on her bed, her prods urging staff to intervene. Later, the kids began only listening to Faith and praised her. 'You saved her life! Oh my god!' Margaret's attacker was immediately reprimanded and sent away and later charged with a felony. The women who murdered Faith currently walk free."

Tenika is then called next to confirm parts of the narrative being ascertained by the jury.

"You are saying that the very following day, the staff grew tired of the kid residents fawning over Faith's achievements, her track race buzz, budding romance with tall, dark, and handsome Michael, her regular hair treatments, from cornrows with extension weavings being kept by her new resident friends. I have that correct, Mrs. Sanders?"

"Y-yes, sir," Tenika stammers. "The largest 300-pound staffer, Wanda, took Faith's Walkman away by ripping the headphone out her ear; I was the only one who witnessed Faith's restraint and murder."

I noticed that Tenika was mentioned to have been on the 911 phone call in court transcripts, but the prosecutor refused to play the evidence. The decision to save the Catholic Diocese of Cleveland over the Parmadale facility was already made, my mom predicted, although I had a smidgen of hope, that maybe we'd see justice be done.

The prosecutor's nonchalant demeanor was infuriating; I grit my teeth to listen for the tidbits of knowledge coming from a nightmare I couldn't wake up from.

What I gathered in the midst of my face warming with tears from the prosecutor's recount was, "Basically, then Faith said something like, 'Duh, I have music privileges,' when she tried to take her Walkman from her, sitting on the couch next to the nine-year-old Talia, who had grown to become Faith's play-sister. And the staffer immediately leaped into an authoritative roar, yanking headphones and calling her coworkers in, saying, 'You've just lost your day! Talking back will not be accepted. You were given a direct order to return the item, and that's that!' The three women then ambushed Faith and tackled her to the ground, slamming her chest into the thinly covered indoor-outdoor carpeted concrete floors."

A silent pause, and Tenika's voice warbled, but she confirmed.

The defense attorney interjected, "Objection! Hearsay. A crunch was heard and a guttural groan underneath the women's bourgeoning weight; in a sweat-filled huff, she called the assistant Ebony to move all the kids into the basement."

"I'll allow it," the judge uttered, and the prosecutor continued.

"You say all of the kids were locked in there for almost two hours. Until finally you, Tenika, broke out, passed Faith's body still laying in the hallway, a stream of bloody vomit leading to her wilted braids."

"Her face was losing oxygen and blood and turning blue," Tenika recounted. "I felt her wrist and then gasped because I saw Wanda still sitting in a chair, watching Faith. I screamed, 'Don't you see she's right there! She's bleeding, I think, and barely moving! Somebody help now!' But she just slowly said, 'If she can talk, she can breathe.' Faith always said she wanted to be an actress. I figure she's probably just acting."

A hollow gasp could be heard from the jury in the silent room.

"My blood ran cold; I could see my friend turning blue. I… I just darted for the office and barricaded in. Just yelling like, '911 get to Parmadale quick; a girl is not breathing. We need help!'" Tenika finished with her voice almost breaking. I felt numb.

"No further questions," the prosecutor said, looking discouraged at the empathy of Cleveland jurors.

And the rest is Faith Finley's legacy. Her death led to a law banning face-down restraints in residential facilities in the state of Ohio after the two-year trial officially wrapped in 2010.

The women were not charged. Never did a single day in jail. Their government job protected them, yet we all are held accountable for our own actions on every level.

But Faith's cause lives on. To always carry a fiery Faithy spirit in you. Don't forget your morals even when life breaks your heart. Because I carry her in my heart. I carry her heart within my own heart.

And in her friend and former roommate Margaret's words: no one can ever tell me Faith's death wasn't about race. The trial was over, but our new lives without Faith had only begun.

CHAPTER 33:

Leaving Foster Care, Moving to Warren

Eventually, despite my adamant protests against the idea, the decision was made for me to go back to Warren with my aunt Ella and cousins and give the family thing a shot. Maybe now that it was a dire circumstance, this would be what brought us together. A couple of weeks later, I was moved back to Warren, and surely enough, as the weeks went by, my cousins started ostracizing me again. More so, Layla and Tori, even Jalisa and Gale, while my cousin JayJay and Uncle Jerry seemed to still have empathy for me. I was obviously conflicted about living with them, as the back-and-forth ridicule of our being homeschooled and overtly Christian had made our athletically egotistical cousins bristle with rage and cruel taunts. Yet even still the first few weeks were okay, Aunt Ella enrolled me into a school called Life Skills, a recommendation from the staff at the foster care facility I was leaving, to better "ease me back into society," they said.

My aunt was insistent that I decided to style my hair I'd wear in an unsettled, natural sort of curly coif. I was quickly taken to a salon to get my hair permed like Layla's, but I refused, insisting on keeping my natural curls but agreeing to a professional flat iron style. My natural curls that my mother has once nurtured and put into twists.

"But Layla's got that cute Rihanna bob cut goin' you should get hip, honey!" the stylist quipped with an impromptu hip pop.

I refused to follow the trend, though, so as not to waste all of my mother's painstaking attempts at caring for my once luminous hair naturally.

Here in Warren, living in the same house where my mother's stepfather beat her felt like an ironic sort of torture, especially being estranged from them for so long. I decided I'd try to just be invisible, and maybe they'd let me grieve and not leave my room unless it was for school. Yet as the weeks went by, they seemed, my cousins especially, quickly got tired of my constant morose and depressed state. One day, I remember my cousin Gale, fed up with my constant crying, rushed me and jumped onto my back, hitting me, taunting me, and laughing and refusing to get off me. I screamed and screamed until my uncle Jerry came flooding into the room, giving him a harsh scolding. I knew that his punishment would only make things harder down the road.

Sometimes, after school and basketball practice, I'd notice a fourteen-year-old JayJay in the dimly lit living room with Aunt Ella under a cloud of smoke that smelled weird and made me nauseous and then horrified realized my aunt was allowing him to smoke weed with her. Smoking marijuana as early as twelve years old for no medical reason seemed beyond foolish of her in my sheltered eyes. Especially because my cousin JayJay was a gifted athlete who later went on to join the Army and almost being kicked out for the same reason: weed. Smoking didn't seem like it would do him any good.

"You let him smoke weed?" I asked quietly.

She scoffed before saying, "It's better to let Jalisa drink with her boyfriend downstairs and for JayJay to smoke with me than let 'em do it out on the streets. And for the record, none of my kids are dead for all the religious mumbo jumbo your mom preaches."

I left the room with tears burning my eyes.

A memory of when I was ten one time and my other aunt Sharon had visited Aunt Ella, one time when Faith and I were in from out of town. My spoiled cousin Tariq, Sharon's son, was used to talking back to my quiet and docile aunt Sharon, whom he had witnessed his own father and her longtime boyfriend, big Antwan (who had refused to marry her) leave her in a pool of her own blood before, quiet as our family kept it and would go off sneaking to listen to C-Murder music as early as seven, memorizing the violent lyrics religiously, while his mother, my aunt Sharon, screamed for him to do chores among other things.

As kids, while we were playing Mario Cart, and it became my turn, Antwan yanked the controller away from me, muttering, "Oh well," and an explicit name under his breath, and in an instant, I felt my heart sink, then felt my face flushing hot with embarrassment as my cousins looked on, seeing red, I flew into a rage. I was ten and sheltered and had never been cursed at before and was humiliated that the first time was by my so-called family.

To him, being desensitized to profanity wasn't a big deal, but to me, it was heartbreaking. I remember tackling him onto the couch and beating his head into the cushions, screaming, "How dare you! You stupid animal! Have some respect for women!"

Everyone was surprised as they pulled me off him; they couldn't believe that I had resorted to violence, and I was partially just as shocked as they were. The normally composed and stoic Jordan they knew was gone. I guess after years of bottling up the chaos at home and the tensions between them had finally taken a head.

At Aunt Ella's, the day for our visit to Ohio State to visit Jalisa and for Gale to enter the basketball regionals had arrived, and I was hoping they'd just let me stay home.

But I was at my rigid aunt Ella's mercy, so of course, it wasn't allowed. The cramped car ride with all four of my cousins, loudly whooping and hollering like always felt like torture. I silently replayed this memory and memories in foster care when I had been forced into random fights and had won, in my head, to endure.

Once we arrived at Jalisa's posh apartments, we were met by Aunt Sharon's brood, my cousin Tariq, Adrian, Dani, and even a distant cousin they called little Antwan. I could see in Antwan's cruel smirk at my arrival that he was not going to make my stay easy.

During the basketball game at the Ohio State basketball regionals, I remember sitting in the hallway for what felt like an eternity, still reeling over Gale's animalistic attack of him jumping on me a few days ago and refusing to support him.

My aunt Ella, with her closely shaved head and power suit and heels, came clacking towards me with her brash brand of confidence built on an ego my grief-stricken state couldn't relate to. She, seemingly reading this attitude in my eyes, said, "Why don't you try to be a part of this family? You know, actin' like this is only gonna make it harder for your cousins to relate to you."

I retorted, "Since when have they ever really cared about relating to me? I've always been an outcast because of history with my mom, which is not even my fault. Even with my twin rotting in the ground won't change that."

"You know that's not true," she retorted before taking me back to the auditorium. Events to come would prove quite the contrary to her lofty hopes of rebuilding our strained family bond on the heels of Faith's sudden death.

Back at Jalisa's apartments and coming off of an apparent loss, the room was in low spirits. I sat quietly, waiting to borrow my cousin Layla's cell phone to call my mom. Antwan came into the room and kept glaring at me, to which I replied with a disgusted look and an eye-roll.

At that, he started going on with a story. "You know, I saw on the news the other day that there's a serial killer out on the loose in Columbus. He has been out here slicing up negros to death," he said with a huge cackle and silent snickers from my cousins. He continued,

"We should send Jordan out there if he comes round here. Her sister is already dead anyway." He snarled and smiled a sinister smile. My heart sank, and I felt the blood drain from my face. I looked at my cousins, for someone, anyone to show a smidgen of compassion, but my cousin Dani just stared at me blankly, waiting for me to resort to desperate violence and, to my heartbreak, said nothing.

At that moment, I gripped the couch corners so as not to cry. I prayed. Surprised my old belief was emerging in this hot seat moment. "Lord, please don't. Don't let me cry here. Not in front of him. Not now. Don't let me give him satisfaction. Oh God, I pray one day that You make him feel this level of despair he's so carelessly put on me."

My prayer seemed to work because my tears seemed to dry up, and a few minutes later, I rose up in a huff and started banging on my aunt Ella's room. She had locked herself in there for some reason. She finally opened it and said, "What, Jordan?" in a harsh and uncaring voice, further fueling my anger.

"You see what your pathetic ego has caused? This so-called cousin of mine mocked my sister while she rots on the ground. You had the nerve to ask me why I didn't want to live with you. This is why! What kind of mother would support her kids doing drugs? I hate all of you. Just send me back!"

My aunt's face became flushed with embarrassment and guilt, and with her voice warbling, she cried, "When I pushed those kids out of my cooch, I made sure they would have everything I never had! Maybe we weren't right on some things, but how dare you! Layla, let her use your phone so she can call her mom. I need to be alone."

Later, in relaying this back to my mom on the phone, I remember her scoffing, saying, "Ha, out of her cooch, sounds just as vulgar and idiotic as she is."

Later, after that harsh exchange of words with Antwan at Ohio State, I resolved in my mind to try my best to mend things with my other cousins despite my growing despair and depression they couldn't relate to. Maybe I could still salvage the relationships I was closer to, like my cousin Dani.

CHAPTER 34

Visit to Aunt Sharon's, Attempt to Re-Bond with Dani After Trauma

A month or so later, I went to visit my aunt Sharon to get a break from life at Aunt Ella's. My cousin Dani was having a get-together of sorts with a friend, and she invited me to come along.

We started venturing toward one of her other friends, Cami, a biracial butterfly they called her. She looked very similar to Dani, and her Natalie Portman-esque features that I would always compare her to. Cami's house was a mini-mansion in Warren, walking there in the summer breeze. Eventually, the party ensued. Before the party, I was even dancing on the floor, showing Cami some of my club moves that I had learned unbeknownst to Dani at that time. It was a supreme shock for Dani to see me rebelling so vigorously from the Christian walk. Cami and her other friend, Ingrid, the ebony to Dani and Cami's ivory, seemed impressed by the performance while Dani was still aghast, not knowing that side of me, the rebellious side.

Anyway, it came time for the boys to come in. At the time, I was seventeen, about to turn eighteen; Dani was fifteen, going on sixteen; and the other girl, Cami, was actually twelve, lying that she was fourteen.

The boys came in, blunts in mouth, bringing in hard liquor like crown apple and other things, and I ended up calling my aunt Emma, who I was staying with at the time. She restricted my mall trip to three hours with Kate from Life Skills the prior week, so I sardonically thought she'd like this new, responsible role I was assuming.

I called, annoyed at their behavior, saying, "Hey, like these kids are drinking over here acting crazy, and I'm the oldest, and I'm not gonna be held responsible; I just wanna go home." I was emotionally distressed and overthinking, and, unfortunately, Dani never really understood my fright at seeing her indulge in such a dangerous activity at such a young age. Even after the shock of Faith's murder was still ringing in all our ears, she refused to fully forgive me, but I felt that real family would be able to have empathy for another family member suffering from severe trauma and grief, no matter the old tensions from family members that don't really involve either party.

These moments would, a few years later, encourage a prodigal daughter rebellion of sorts in the years after my sister's homicide, from nineteen to twenty. A Christian girl's positive ambition and outlook gone sour to rotten. The will to live while hating God turned into a mission of being as disturbing as possible to repel as many "fake" or Type-A type of people as possible, giving the middle finger to suburbia and embracing my inner diva.

Acrylic gel nails, elaborate sew-in weaves, new reasons to shop for new high-end corsets and lingerie, literally getting paid instantly to catwalk prance around in all day while guys literally drool over you, became my reality and felt like a dreamy, passionate another world I got to escape into. I saw a movie about a girl who went from jail to exotic dancing and found a sense of freedom by dancing bare and letting her inhibitions go. In foster care's secured treatment center felt like a jail I had been forced into, and the exotic dancing circuit became the escape from everything: from the drama with my mom, my stepsister, my slain twin sister, the trial, everything. Later, I would always come running back to the church and the foot of the cross going through college, but not until much later would the glitz wear off and my desire for God, through rejections and ending bonds, make me realize that Jesus is the most real friend you can have.

A prayer for when I miss the mark:

> *"Jesus wasted Himself for the world. I can waste some time in prayer just like I have wasted my most precious pearls before swine. Lord, I am sickened to my stomach and mad at myself for giving in. Lord, please cleanse me and purify me. Take my heart and make it over, Lord, because I love You. You're my soul, my life, my source of everything, the reason why I live each day. In Jesus' name, amen and amen."*

Before the glitz wore off, the drama followed me there. For a little while, it felt like I had a new power over my life. The power to decline a client, the power to expect a stack of either twenty or fifty-dollar bills for a twenty-minute conversation, to leave with close to $1,000 for four hours of work, was a rush.

The fact that not every lady who tries out is picked gives an upper-echelon feel to the dance world. Learning the art of conversation. More like subtlety schmoozing Tom, Dick, or Harry, a moderately attractive middle-aged working dude, or whoever.

A "regular" client to a hustling girl.

I never really learned more than two or three pole moves; the attempt kept me in shape like no other. Nights with twenty-dollar bills pouring out of my purse felt exciting. It was a rush to see how much attention you could get.

But also awful for someone as emotionally sensitive as I truly am underneath the makeup.

Especially the choir girl turned stripper baddie by night.

It was part of the exhibitionist in me, the daredevil, that three-year-old baby that dove into a twelve-foot-deep blue pool and floated down in amazement as my sixteen-year-old Russian stepsister dove in after me, understandably in a panic.

It was that seven-year-old girl with Brandy Microbraids and Scary Spice platform shoes who said, "Yeah! I wanna go on the fasted ride at Cedar Point!" And did. Not even truly tall enough for the ride, my Russian stepdad John holding me into my seat as my braids reached for the sky, my body was lifting out of the Millennium Force 2000 rollercoaster.

Then the basement belly dance classes I paid for to add an artistic element to my style of dance and presentation.

Watching *Memoirs of a Geisha* and my mother giving me her copy of the novel as an assignment, overworked yet still brilliant.

It was that fearless, innately wildly courageous girl, floating and soaring simultaneously between dreams and reality, holy fire coursing in her veins with wild hope. It was that girl's God-given gifts that propelled me into the exotic dancing circuit. I emphasize the God-given aspects of gifts that I was giving to the world as a cautionary part of my story for a girl reading this to never be encouraged to have a mysterious double life or rebel stage. It's not worth the regret or wasted potential you have in Christ and for internal peace. I emphasize this point to help you understand that the love for music, zest, and passion that arises in your heart was placed there for a reason.

That passion that keeps you up at night was given to you for a reason, and that reason is that it was sent and made by God. Don't squander your pearls before swine, running away from grief. I emphasize this point to remind you that even in the face of very real grief and the depths and lows that depression and mental bondage can take you to, a girl with holy fire in her veins can still fight for that dream that seems "yes, I believe it and have seen myself being it in my mind, but it's really not for me" that that is a lie from the pit of hell.

If a dream was placed in your heart, then it was placed there by the creator, and no weapon formed against it should prosper.

If you're a girl or young adult facing your worst fears and hope to gain or learn from a girl who survived, just know she did not give up. Even if you have made some similar prodigal mistakes, it's never too late to stoke the embers of your own Holy Spirit and the holy fire that fuels the flame.

Never give up. For what can you learn as the black sheep, the underdog, the backslider, whatever you want to call it, if all they give you is toxic positivity or pity parties? You can absolutely learn from a censored, prim, and proper housewife's testimony despite going through personal hardships in your life that they most likely can't really relate to or speak to. You can learn how to clip and tailor your mind and speech patterns and eventually become religious and uptight and let the holy fire simmer down. Or you can learn from a pioneer in women's rights, following a more relatable path to yours, who has made mistakes and repented, on how to not let the ugliness in the world kill the God-given goodness left in you.

CHAPTER 35:

Grief and Rebel Stage Mindset Continued

Later, I created a very real and raw art visual representation of the transformations I was going through before moving closer toward stability.

At the height of my rebellion, I felt compelled to photograph the moments during everything, mainly big moments, but also the hard moments. During the makeup application in the bathroom breaking down, I just thought someday if I just made myself into art, someone would finally notice and give me a career. I was between nineteen and twenty-one, and thinking things out was not the wave.

Crazily enough, now I can say that I truly am thankful for those bathroom night breakdowns, where in the middle of applying a liquid eyeliner from Sephora, I'd fumble it nearly down the drain. The smudge would cause me to pause and then stop. Grunt, reflect, and stare into tears. Then pray. Give up enough to pray.

I'm glad I listened to those little nudges to photograph everything; even the faintest whisper of faith was enough for the Holy Spirit to gently guide the identity He made me for while I was trying to decorate and erase myself into my own mural of metamorphosis.

Later, it would make my words burst into the reader's heart and (some) of the new faces mentioned along the way, but mostly my own.

But I needed to see that I could go completely away from Him, yet come back, admit, and submit to His ways over mine.

I needed to see that I had that same grace.

The grace of Rahab. Remember Rahab's ministry. How before the Israelites crossed the Jordan, Joshua sent men to scout out the land. Arriving in Jericho, they decide to spend the night at the house of the prostitute named Rahab. When Jericho's ruler tries to apprehend them, Rahab hides them and then helps them escape through the window, thus saving their lives.

Later, after the book of Joshua, Rahab is mentioned in the Bible in the opening chapter of the book of Matthew, where we find her in the genealogy of Jesus Christ.

God can give you the grace of Rahab, the lowest in the caste system, exalted to the heights of an unfading crown. I'm thankful there's a God so redeeming that He would deliver me from carnal desires... and, after severe trauma, be able to show someone else what that process truly looks like.

Wiping off the makeup, washing out the product in your hair. And learning to love that person underneath it all.

#DieToSelf #LiveForChrist #RahabMinistries.

I chose to dance for about half a year to stoke my artistic fire without adding the holy at first, then realized that if you're chosen, there's no running away from it. Things will continue to not work out for you because you can serve God or money. You can't serve God and money. You can serve one or the other.

> *No man can serve two masters: for either he will hate the one, and love the other; or else he will hold to the one, and despise the other. Ye cannot serve God and mammon.*
>
> — Matthew 6:24–26 (KJV)

If you don't repent, things will continue to not work out for you in the area you want God to move in most, while it does for everyone else because chosen ones are rare for a purpose. To show that with or without rebellion, tragedy can strike. Better to be prepared on God's side than on Satan's when the shock of suffering hits you. Whenever I leave somewhere, I want to be like thank God that person, man, or woman, taught me how to fight for life and even in Christ too, so an extra win.

CHAPTER 36:

Turning Eighteen.
Surviving the Shock of
Homicide

It wasn't too long after that harsh exchange of words at Columbus and Dani's party before things finally came to a head in living with my extended family in Warren. I was sent back to Berea Children's Home a month or so after that dispute, yet it wasn't merely because my aunt said, "Get out," but mainly due to my own misery and impulsive actions that came flooding out one day. Born out of quiet desperation of needing to be loved and heard by my mother, who, despite all of this pain and suffering, still was waiting in the balance, yearning to be met.

One time, during a monitored visit with my mom, I accidentally let it slip out about my cousin JayJay being allowed to smoke weed while my every move was closely monitored and restricted. I think I was lamenting about the incident in Columbus, the overbearing control over where I went with a few friends I had made at Life Skills, and slights from Jalisa on my weight gain and Layla refusing to do chores and putting it on me when it slipped out.

My mom seemed to be so enraptured with my friend Candace's homestead, whom she had brought along to our visit, and rather aloof to my woes, much to my dismay and building enragement. Whenever things were tense with Faith or me, my mom would pick one of our school friends to start mothering and showering with attention; I think in part to show us how ungrateful we were in her eyes and how much our friends loved her doting on them.

Most of our friends were only around for the thrift store shopping sprees and motherly cuddles that they didn't get at home, yet when it became time to lay down the law, she'd bark her orders at us and resort to the humiliation ritual she had done to us with our cousins.

The game of picking one of our school friends to start mothering and showering with attention manifested with some of our friends; she had even lived with us for part of the school year when we lived in Wooster for a few years.

History seemed to be repeating itself with the savior act again while disregarding my word. My mom seemed to be so enraptured with Candace's homestead, who she brought along to our visit, and who she had begun spending a lot of time and partially even living with. I met Candace in seventh grade in Wooster, one of my only friends besides Asia. Candace has a biracial half-sister and seemed to relate to my plight in the very judgmental and racist old-fashioned town of Wooster and the treatment I got. Yet, now, here my mom was, once again hogging my friends and getting involved in her family issues. Candace had also just found out she was pregnant, which further ramped up my mother's savior complex. *All the better to distract her with*, I thought darkly. A nice distraction from her own daughter's murder trial and her living daughter's upsetting living situation.

"Oh, Mommy. Remember how we got sick from the buffet and had to pull over to unbutton our pants!" Candace said, trying to lighten the mood. "Oh, yes! Haha. I even took a picture of you taking a breather on the highway!"

"You're an outrageous one, Candy," my mom said, completely disregarding me bringing up the incident with Antwan and Aunt Ella in Columbus.

My irritation grew, and desperate to get my issues acknowledged, I brought up, "Ha, yeah. You two are having the time of your lives while

I have to be controlled, and my backpack smells like weed and their moldy old house every day," embittered.

The older black lady who had been silently taking notes said, "What weed smoke? In the home. I'm sorry, Jordan, but I'll have to report this."

I tried backtracking, but it was too late. Back I went to Berea after a dramatic consultation between Ella and me, her not believing my accident and me hurriedly throwing things in garbage bags.

"Just like the way you came in," she taunted as I left with a caseworker.

I stayed in a girls' group home way out in the grassy country in New Philadelphia for a year, and through all the drama that went on there, I somehow survived to eighteen. Back in Akron, my mom's civil lawsuit lawyer, Jill Flagg, had also become my mother's latest daughter project and had somehow even convinced Jill to let her live in an old property of hers in Firestone Park. A house she and her husband lived in while she finished law school and he medical school. My mother, grandmother, Candace, my stepsister Allie and teenaged Melody and her other son and daughter I didn't know as well, along with Jill and even my youth minister Mrs. Patty Neidert, all greeted me with a welcome back party in the sunny living room. A welcome banner and cake and balloons and a playhouse for the kids in the backyard surprised me when I walked in, and tears came to my eyes. Tears that Faith wasn't here for it. I relished the gifts and belated eighteenth birthday celebration for the moment, yet somehow, I knew that this version of my mother wouldn't last.

My mom and I started working to reconcile our strained bond and adjust to this new normal. Spike, my noble little fox terrier boy, was back, but I even noticed he seemed rattled and shaken. His beagle sister Macy, more high maintenance than him, was gone, and so was his second momma, Faith. He often slept in Faith's old clothes and would come up to me whimpering, his big, innocent eyes pleading as if he were asking me where she was. It broke my heart and sent me into a fit of tears and wails that would last for hours. Seeing the loss in my sweet little dog and not being able to explain it to him or myself felt unbearable.

In a step toward healing, my mom, not being able to take my days of uncontrollable sobs and even fainting times, had come up with the idea to donate some money in Faith's name. The legal case we had lost, the homicide ruling stayed but was classified as accidental, but the civil lawsuit we'd won in the ruling of a wrongful death lawsuit in 2008.

The foster care facility, Parmadale, was officially closed in 2010 as a result of the negative press surrounding my sister's wrongful death homicide case.

CHAPTER 37:

Interlude

My mother donated a large sum of money from her settlement to our on-and-off "home church" Liberty Tabernacle in Akron. The church started out as a small storefront and, in its heyday, had expanded large enough to build a larger church in the spaciousness of Barberton. Faith and I would always connect to a church and join the choir wherever we were in our many journeys of moves.

The church building was member-funded and also built by the pastor and some church members who had a background in carpentry, so extending funds to establish a church kitchen, naming it "Faith's Kitchen," and holding a ceremony felt like God was carving a way for us to establish beauty in Faith's name, even in the midst of our agony of losing her.

However, my mother's idea started in 2010, once I was finally out of foster care, but it wouldn't be brought to fruition until I pleaded and begged and demanded her to follow through with it in 2016.

In those six years that followed, an unbelievable whirlwind of events took place, as the ups and downs of both of our mental health took a toll on our mother-daughter bond until we officially last saw each other in 2016, but more on that later.

The biggest point I want to make is that it's only by the grace of God that I lived through it all to be able to tell the tale. I truly hope and pray that through someone reading my story they may hold onto their own loved ones longer when they hug them, tighter in their embrace, more viscerally, more intimately, more heartfelt. While we all have God who chose to rely on His salvation, we must learn to love each other in a Christ-like way. For your very life and everything you hold dear depends on it.

CHAPTER 38:

Notable Abridgment

As a result of winning the wrongful death civil lawsuit, a law banning face-down restraints in residential areas became known as the Faith Finley law following the end of the homicide trial officially two years after Faith's death (2008), in 2010. I'm so thankful that I have photos of Faith in her Barack Obama t-shirt that we got at Michelle Obama's speech at North High School in Akron, Ohio, in late 2007. Even with little resources, my mom was still fighting to pour knowledge into us. Moments like this followed by one of our last family moments, seeing the historical black history play *A Raisin in the Sun* at the Akron Civic Theatre and my mom driving us to Hudson to see the Shakespeare play in the park, *The Taming of the Shrew*, etc. She had been reading to us in the safety and solitude of the suburban women's shelter hidden within grassy forested neighborhoods.

CHAPTER 39:

Making It to Eighteen & Moving into P.A.L. Missions Girl's Group Home, College and Beyond

This time, it would be on my own, after just laying down my twin sister to rest at her funeral service. It was a large white ranch-style house for foster youths to transition from teenager to adulthood.

A huge stone estate known as the P.A.L. Mission house was nestled in the middle of the grassy countryside, with three stories, walk-in closets, a basement recreation room, a large kitchen and dining area, nooks and crannies for quiet time, and with a small lake in the backyard, reminding me of Twin Lakes. It looked like a place where a girl moving in could be viewed favorably despite being dubbed a *troublemaker* in the foster care system.

I was greeted by the foster directors, later to be known as the foster aunties, Wendy and Sharon, in front of the pleasantly lit entrance and then by at least three girls with *Twilight* books in tow, ready to show me the ropes of the place. We ended up making "peace signs" with our index and middle fingers until it created a "star" shape amongst the three of us; the rocker girl Trisha would become my closest friend during my stay.

Next, I met Shaneka, Cherrelle, Latoya, and Brittany, who, according to Shaneka, ran the house. I could tell by their no-nonsense tone of voice that they thought they were honorary staff members, but I liked their air of confidence and independence.

As I was unpacking my things and getting settled into my new bed and room, shared by two other girls, I hung up some newer shirts I had just gotten from Gabriel Brothers when Shaneka came rushing into my room exclaiming, "Ooh, girl, you got a *lot* of clothes! You only got one clothes voucher like us, right?"

"Yeah, I just shopped in clearance because you get the most bang for your buck that way."

"Ah, smart," Shaneka retorted quickly, eyeballing tee shirts and picking up a couple. "Can I have this one? Here, I'll trade you for another one. I'll be right back!" she squealed before I could reply and was off.

Even though the staff members warned about sharing things and then wanting them back, I was seventeen going on eighteen, and Shaneka was only fourteen; I figured if she had anything to trade, I'd see what it was and go from there.

She came back with a few cute tops, one that was multicolored, one that was very worn, and a plain black tank top that I wanted to wear under my shirts.

I agreed to trade with her for one tee shirt, and although she looked a little dissatisfied that she didn't get more, I knew an alliance had been formed.

Down in the basement lounge was where the head director of P.A.L., Kayla, welcomed me and one other new girl named Hailey into the house with the other foster girls.

"We help our girls learn basic home living skills like cooking, cleaning, and holding a job, as you know, Jordan, from the other P.A.L.

in Kent. I'm explaining more for Hailey's sake, she just came from her home to our boarding. You'll find that here, our rules are still the same, but being out in the countryside like we are, you'll have an opportunity to pass cow farms on our nightly walks, learn a new independence skill each week, and prep for your upcoming high school diploma test, or the GED. As long as you can try to make our job easier, your stay here should go smoothly.

"For instance, Cherelle just learned how to cook her third meal here, and the meal times rotate between all nine of you girls a week," she continued.

Cherelle chimed in with, "I already know how to cook; y'all ain't teach me that much, dang. You makin' us sound like we little kids or something," and the room erupted in silent giggles.

"That's not to say that some of you haven't come with your own independent life skills like you, Cherelle; you are a great cook, actually. You know what I mean; I'm just introducing our new housemates to how P.A.L. Mission works. Be nice, Cherelle," Kayla replied, giving her a knowing smirk.

I ended up staying there for seven months, and the fun memories and dramatic memories are distant but not too far from mind.

In those months, I realized that the people you meet in your life, regardless of what circumstances brought you there, everyone has something to teach you.

Trisha taught me how to dig up our own worm bait and that you could make a fishing pole out of long sticks, a lone wire, and a hook and still catch dozens of fish in our pond on days when missing Faith would overwhelm me.

Brittany taught me how to thrive at a graduation ceremony even if your supporters aren't related by blood to you. She also taught me how to coexist with someone who has control issues like she did. Shaneka taught me how to face my fears of confrontation and to speak up for myself even when I didn't want to. Cherelle and Latoya were an inseparable duo and taught me how to strive to relate to others who are the same race as me, but different than me.

Even though we were all black young women, our lives and growing up had been vastly different from each other's. We all grew up fast, though, so we could relate to that fact. The house seemed to inevitably split into the four black girls versus the five white girls' cliques, as even the nice house couldn't overshadow the darkness that racial tensions would bring out.

In spite of those relational tensions, all in all, the P.A.L. Mission house stood as a place where the girls had bonded with the hard-working staff members, whom they affectionately called "the aunties" sheltered and helped raise them during a time when circumstances in their own family were on shaken ground. Those precious years had created a debt none of the girls could ever hope to repay. Consider donating to these foster house programs because they were a beacon of hope during bleak times, and I feel that they deserve more recognition.

Some in-house romances would follow, but I never let myself get caught up in that; I was more focused on my GED and trying to get back home to Mommy.

What P.A.L. Mission Girl's Group Home taught me was how to survive when I felt like each new breath into this new normal without my twin would be my undoing.

In retrospect, through the loud girl fight arguments, good memories of pool parties, and bouts of manic-depressive episodes met with immediate wise and understanding foster aunties. Between the family dinners and the therapy of having the foster aunties readily available for a pep talk whenever I needed them, I'm so grateful that I had those wonderful women at a time when I needed to decompress from anxiety about Faith's homicide.

The P.A.L. Mission house is for a lot of girls, and even me, a second chance at life. A place for me to feel secure amongst the grassy countryside, visiting cows and even some pet tigers owned by neighboring friends. For the rest of that year, I worked out the beginning stages of grieving my twin Faith, but also in carving out a new life for myself. Once I turned eighteen, I completed my General Education Diploma (GED) and picked up a new job at Marc's grocery store.

The changes from the girls' group home to living back with my mom were jarring, but by the grace of God, I started to adjust.

Surprisingly enough, years later, at twenty-one, I enrolled in the University of Akron and attempted to connect with my cousin Layla (per my aunt's request), who had just started there. I got a part-time job at a beauty supply store in Akron called KP Beauty. The surprise came when I saw my cousin Antwan there, working at the adjacent Kicks shoe store next door. He never mentioned the taunting remarks he made towards me in Columbus, and I assumed some maturity had entered his life, so I decided not to bring it up.

One day after work, Antwan asked me for a ride home. I felt a brief sear of anger rise up in me at the audacity of the oh-so-confident Antwan, who felt cocky enough to taunt me days after I had buried my twin sister, but I decided to be the bigger person and relented.

Yet, instead of praying it off and truly using the opportunity to witness the restorative peace of Jesus Christ, I had slowly begun on a dark path of smoking weed and partying hard to prove to my cousins that I was just as fearless as them. I taunted him by blasting the "Panda" song that had just come out by Designer to rub it in his face that he was relying on someone he considered weak to get him home.

Anyway, about a year later, I saw news articles of Antwan's face being plastered all across Facebook, then went to my aunt's page to confirm it. Antwan had been selling heroin and fentanyl to college kids while we were working together and had sold a fatal dose to his girlfriend at the time. He was sentenced to thirteen years in prison because it was ruled as a double homicide as the girl was pregnant, not with his child, the autopsy would come to find. The guy who had been my tormentor and had gotten the seal of approval from my ever-so-cool and street-wise cousins was the guy who was responsible for taking the life of a young and impressionable woman.

I felt God's voice silently telling me to repent before I ended up the same way. Even in my rebellious stage away from Him, His Holy Spirit was still witnessing to me.

Reminding me of how we do not battle against flesh and blood, but against principalities and spirits of wickedness. And the reason why he was accepted by my harsh cousins, and I wasn't, was because of this fact. Their spirit was and is ultimately heartless and wicked. It also felt like an eerie premonition of the power that prayer holds, especially in the name of Jesus.

In utter shock, I closed the news article. I saw the young girl he had inadvertently murdered was a white girl. I also remember seeing Antwan's mugshot on Google news, his beautiful, handsome face and hazel eyes staring into the line, and just thinking silently that even if he was my half-cousin, he was still my cousin in my blood and, therefore, one-half of me. I read that it was noted in his court documents that he had cried on the stand, demonstrating remorse uncommon in cold-blooded killers, during the end of his trial, when surviving family members of his then-girlfriend made their testimonies, so there is still hope for him. I hope that maybe he can see this one day and remember that even in his worst days, he helped me fight for life in my worst moment.

Yet the women who killed Faith never did a day in jail. As they were public service workers for a government-run facility, they were protected by the Catholic Diocese of Cleveland as staff workers, so they were not penalized or held accountable for what they deemed a wrongful death lawsuit regarding my twin sister's heinous murder.

The quote that Fox News got of my mother saying, "If Faith had been blond-haired and blue-eyed, she would've gotten justice," rang in my ears. The wave of terror at how close to home the cruelty of my family was to me sent a repented spirit in my heart.

After dropping Antwan off, we'd see each other passing at work. He even asked me for a ride to the family reunion, but I was planning on taking my then-boyfriend/fiancé, Mark, and he quickly revoked his request. I didn't think anything of it. The dinner and reunion were great; my aunts seemed relieved I had a new storyline and were intrigued with Mark's tall stature, former Marine Corps story, and chiseled, Germanic features reminiscent of a Tommy from the melo-dramatic TV show *Power* type. To my strikingly handsome former NFL player cousin in town for a visit, Marlo Manningham, and Tori's graduation party, I stood silently at first as Mark smiled wryly, trying to maintain his confidence.

Celebrating Tori's high school graduation came with photo ops my frenzied college mind had accustomed me to organizing.

When we left the party hall and headed back to Ella's, Mark seemed frustrated with me for agreeing to go because of me explaining the past. I was twenty-three, still full of enough hope and positivity to encourage it. Yet sure enough, as we cramped into the familiar kitchen, I saw Mark's flushed look each time they conversationally said "negro." At first, he thought it was about me; I reassured him and felt a flood of panic.

Layla, newly enrolled in college despite eventually dropping out from failing grades despite Marla's school coach scholarship she had sacrificed for Layla. She invites me out to the car to relax, and Tariq's already there, now an adult with a child of his own on the way, to spark a strong joint of weed. We talk and reminisce, and I start getting even more paranoid as I don't know what they're talking about, but I figured they're grilling him with questions and giving him the hot seat. Mark and I had been dating for several months at this point, and he had been bringing up engagement and had given me his Marine Corps ring, with the engravings of the historical battle of Iowa Jima encased in gold and red rubies that he got in Iraq for receiving the Purple Heart award overseas.

Later, in a rage of me taking my stepsister Allie's advice to send it back if I felt that he was rushing me and was not ready. He'd send me a photo of the ring smashed with a hammer before a video of him throwing it into Lake Anna. That was 2016, and nearing the end of the year, I noticed tensions and side-eye glares from my cousins at random when I would visit but decided to shrug it off. College, work, and the fast-paced credit selling pressure of T.J.Maxx made KP Beauty feel like maybe God had Antwan and me there for a healing moment.

CHAPTER 40:

Bad Influences

Ireceived a panicked call from Layla crying hysterically, telling me a modeling agent in Akron had tried assaulting her, and she needed me to come and pick her up immediately.

"Jordan, please! You gotta help me. My car broke down, and these model dudes stole my money. Can you come get me? And they towed me! Antwan doesn't drive, you know that."

"Oh my God, are you okay? Why would you go to a model call by yourself? Uhh, well, I guess I can get you. Isn't there anyone else that can take you to the car lot tomorrow, though? I have to work early in the morning."

She quickly interjected, "No, Jordan. I need you. Plus, you promised my mom you wouldn't let me be alone out here in Akron. Please, just please do this for me. I have nobody out here!"

I sighed and thought, *Well, she'd just need to stay until the morning. It would inconvenience me, but maybe my help would lighten her up in the future.* I reluctantly obliged and rushed to go find her at some random apartment buildings.

She hopped in the car giddily, sparking up a small joint, saying, "Wow, you saved my life. Don't tell my mom, er, Aunt Ella, promise?"

Later on, I guess Layla assumed that it'd be like our freshman pothead days, but I was on a strict schedule and on the merit roll, so I went to bed. In the flurry to try to get Layla to the dealership in the morning and back to work, the Korean family who owned it didn't accept my reasoning, and Antwan wasn't there for me to even try to appeal to him. It was a swift, curt, and hurtful instant firing that I was blindsided by. Was it all a cruel setup and a lie to go gloat with Antwan about later? I wouldn't understand this or realize it until years later, but they were both out to get me. I was surprised that my oh-so-tough cousins even saw me as that much of a threat.

Back at home, relaying this all to my mom, who, back from the Caribbean, had lost her Firestone Park home and was living with me in my two-bedroom apartment, I remember her giving me sound advice as she was slowly coming to from quite literally a severe mental breakdown.

After the trial, my mom had been relentless and chaotically spending her money and just being ridiculously spontaneous, from one minute saying she was going to vacation in Pennsylvania to saying she should've married her trucker boyfriend Sean and moved to Atlanta despite his instability.

Now, as I'm trying to pursue my life outside of the tragedy of Faith's passing and my mother's drama, she was coming around. Well, flashes of her. She told me to remember who Layla's mother is, and it didn't really resonate until the last time I saw them in 2020.

CHAPTER 41:

The Dark Path; Rebelling against God, Health Issues from Grief

The years of eighteen to twenty-one years old may have only been three years, but it felt like I had lived ten lifetimes by the end of them. Surely enough, as predicted, my mother's put-together act I'd seen at my belated eighteenth birthday party in July was wavering and splintering as she struggled with her fibromyalgia, grieving Faith's passing away, and finding her place in a new and terrifying world. The world of being the parent of a murdered twin daughter and of a reeling twin-less daughter who was at odds and struggling to stay afloat.

Sean, my mother's wandering truck driver slash entrepreneur boyfriend, had also reemerged from Cincinnati during the trial and during the height of all the hoopla from the Akron beacon journal and press was raging on. Sean was always normally distant and wandering, being on his whirling truck driving schedule. However, he had magically gained the ability to micromanage his truck career while planning on how to turn my Faith's court winnings into an investment for his clothing store in Cincinnati. To add insult to injury, a wedding was also being planned, and hastily so, for the Sheraton in Cuyahoga Falls. Meanwhile, I was still waking up in cold sweats, self-weaning myself off thirteen different medicines I was forced to swallow. Every day, I was doped up on medication in foster care for a major depressive disorder I was diagnosed with there. But at least being back home meant the freedom to quit.

I should've been under the care of a physician and not abruptly stop them all at once, though. If my mom hadn't been so wrapped up in this impulsive wedding, she may have made that distinction. She was so enraptured in her plan for a new life that she only noticed how barely able to function in the aftermath of Faith's homicide I was. It was only when I would have a fit and wake up screaming from nightmares of seeing Faith being killed in different ways and crying out to me in my dreams.

I had also begun spells of suddenly stopping breathing at night; later, I would learn it was sleep apnea, which caused me to stop breathing during sleep. Dreams of seeing Faith's beautiful corpse and cold, hard skin in the morgue filled my nights. Per emergency room doctors' orders, I was to sleep next to my mother every night to make sure she could shake me if I stopped breathing at night.

My mother never slept much before Faith's death, and now it seemed like she never did anymore. Or at least she finally would sleep after a week of manic alertness forced her body to finally pass out in exhaustion. My mom's new California king-sized bed, meant for her life as a newlywed, was now always filled with her heavy Frank Peretti novels and crossword puzzles and some scattered loose-leaf Bible verses she'd scribble at times when she could bear it. Or wasn't cursing God.

A painfully debilitating side effect of quitting the powerful psychotropic drugs that were being administered to me and all the kids from children's services resulted in me temporarily losing nerve control over my bladder. This condition would last for about a year before I got it under control with court-ordered therapy. More on what led the courts to force me into seeing a shrink weekly later.

A year later, at nineteen, after I thought I'd get some respite from my unwarranted urges, I developed an ulcer in my throat that leaked acid, which poured into my stomach. I was unable to eat anything but broth for two months as the invasive surgery in a Caribbean hospital to extract it called for. But at eighteen, the nervous issue would plague me, much to my despair, at almost any given moment of slight pressure.

The new grocery store job at Marc's felt like I was floating through my new normal. I'd walk into the store for my shift feeling like I had a hot air balloon for a head with robot hands making me do the work to later be picked up by Mommy, trying to give me an encouraging smile, only to immediately lose my ability to breath and suddenly barely be able to hold my bladder in, followed by crying and sometimes even throwing up if I got too close to having an accident on myself before I got in the house.

At eighteen, Sean had started slowly trying to move into controlling my mother's life and, more importantly, her newfound finances. I grew enraged at his opportunistic approach and the halted plans for Faith's Kitchen Dedication Ceremony at our home church in Barberton that she had promised me. She'd already donated the ghastly sum of money, and production on the kitchen had begun, but a ceremony for our dear Faith? That seemed out of the question, what with her lavish nuptials and sudden happy ending barging in. No time to avenge her slain daughter's name. Or care about the identical specimen who couldn't bear life without her.

A David's Bridal fitting was hurriedly prepared, and instantly, Allie's kids, my mom, and I were all there being fitted for tuxedos with purple ties and lavender-colored dresses. Eventually, I decided to move into a single-room boarding house to get away from Sean and my mother. However, by November, the job at Marc's took its toll on my fragile state, with several times the ambulance being called to our house because I had stopped breathing in my sleep.

One night, as they loudly planned their wedding, I caught Sean suddenly whispering, telling my mom to send me to a rehab facility until "I get things together." The word facility rang through me like an ominous bell tower and sent my heart into a flurry of rage.

The chaos from foster care was still fresh in my mind. I roared at Sean. Sean was a former footballer with a heavy physique, a tall man at six-foot-three, easily 350 pounds. He looked startled at my sudden outburst but didn't back down. Even going as far as to curse at me.

"It's nobody's fault here your twin got killed, and don't talk to your mother that way!" he roared after I screamed, "I'm not being sent anywhere!"

"Who the hell are you? You were never here all the times you could've bonded with us; you're only here *now* because she's dead! And you want money for your pathetic, broke business that ain't going nowhere. Get the hell outta here!"

"Get the hell out?" he quipped, not missing a beat. "I have family flying into Atlanta for the wedding, and *you* best believe, and after the wedding, we are moving! And yo jerk be lucky to be in my laid-out pad come Christmas, keep talking."

At that instant, I rushed upstairs to where their instant marriage room was cuddled and started throwing his things.

I heard him banging up the stairs.

I saw red. I could barely see what I was doing, but I grabbed a broom at first. Threw it at him. Then grabbed bleach and started sloshing it on his clothes and the carpet, even dousing him on his jeans and leather jacket.

His face flushed red, and he roared, "Toni! Get this girl before I hurt her — no!"

I had the small TV set in my hands and hurled it directly into his groin. I heard his bellowing screams and curses as my mom wailed his name. I flew out of the house while he doubled over in pain.

I ran to Allie's house, who lived about ten blocks away, and camped out there for a week. I came back the next week to a darkened house, my grandma Nana coming in from out of town. The week didn't do much good, though. My mom was fuming mad at me that Sean had fled back home to settle scores with his family before they flew in, weeks away from their shotgun wedding.

"How dare you pull that crazy scene? Jordan, he was about to have you locked up. It took everything in me to stop him! Everything! He had to go to the hospital, you know? You actually sprained his pelvis. Jesus — God… do you want to end up in the morgue, too?" My mom cried.

Annoyed at this random attack, I tried to implore my grandma, but she was catatonic and mute, clearly in terror.

"Yeah, your so-called husband is only here to gouge your daughter's death money! Thanks to you, my beautiful twin is being eaten by maggots right now! You should've died, not her! It's like her life was worthless to you!" I hollered uncontrollably. The rage was overbearing. I felt like I would make good on all my threats to kill myself.

"Jordan, stop it! It's one in the morning, okay? The neighbors will call the cops!" she wailed, not addressing my concerns that her wedding and Faith's ceremony were rather poorly timed.

"The cops? It's because of you and your pathetic delusions of grandeur. Calling the cops like you're some white woman! Knowing you had two beautiful black girls! That you were holding back cause you're a jealous, miserable, weak jerk! Too weak to tell your mommy that she abused you or whatever, ugh! I'm so sick of you!"

I grabbed her flip phone and began to throw it at the wall, but my mom was in my face, so I tossed it on the couch and fled out into the snow, screaming. I screamed outside to myself with no coat. Half walked into traffic to the sound of angry, roaring traffic honks.

About a half hour later, when I was circling back to the house, I saw cop car lights flashing and heard my mother's familiar histrionic shrill saying, "She's gonna get herself killed! She's already threatened me, and she hit me!" lying to the cops yet again.

I protested, but it was no use.

No more than a few short months after burying my slain twin sister, I was now locked in tight handcuffs when I should've been shown some mercy, even despite my lashing out. A new psychiatric hospital hold was long overdue.

My mother lied to the cops to spite me, and I was arrested. Wailing out to God in the paddy wagon. Praying to God for strength to get through this, somehow. "This too shall pass," was a resounding voice I heard ring in my soul. I was grateful that even in this unfortunate circumstance, I could derive comfort from the Holy Spirit, no matter where I was. Next, at the jail, I was strip searched and roughly tackled by at least six policemen before being put in a suicide vest with unsticking Velcro. That Thanksgiving, I spent in a jail cell. I even huffed some bleach I found in a hysteria in an attempt to end it all. I couldn't imagine a holiday in jail, yet there I was with only the resounding words of the Bible, stone walls, and time to reflect on pursuing college and leaving this blunder behind me with help from the probate courts.

CHAPTER 42:

How God Helped Me Defeat Rage!

It took me laying on that ball of fire that went from holy to hellfire and getting my boiling chest and face onto the cooling floor.

If you're in a rageful spirit, the first thing to do is immediately get to the floor. Press yourself face forward until you can feel your heartbeat and feel and count your heart beating back up into your face. Grab something solid that won't break, like a piece of furniture. Then, talk to God. Let your words flow into the blanket or sheet. Cling to that leg of your furniture piece and grit the words out of your teeth.

With tears streaming, teeth gritted, I talked to God, "God… yeah, like You care. Even my tears seem kind of in vain. I hate You for letting me be alive. I don't hate You; I hate the past heartbreak that You didn't spare me from. I didn't do anything wrong to deserve heartbreak, yet here I am. Even the parts of me that did do something bad after the heartbreak… I didn't deserve this… but then again, You didn't deserve it either."

Acknowledging my anger at my circumstances brought me peace. Acknowledging Jesus' suffering brought me peace. I allowed it to wash over me.

Feel the fire in your chest draining away with each word uttered to Jesus.

This is your breakthrough. You're now breaking a generational curse off of you and your life. Your heart is mending. In Jesus' name, I thank You, Lord. Amen and Amen.

My mom eventually came to visit me and put twenty dollars on my books and even attempted to have the domestic violence charge reversed. Due to the growing press surrounding Faith's homicide and Parmadale's stature, I was ordered to attend mental health court for two years of therapy.

My mom came rushing to the courts, begging them to drop the charges, just as she did when I was sent to foster care. Thankfully, I had a merciful African American female judge, and my prayers in jail were answered. I would be shown a smidgen of mercy, given the circumstances of my twin's homicide trial.

The domestic violence misdemeanor charge would only be removed if I completed two years of probation in mental health court. Meanwhile, through the jubilant exchange of Melody showing me Photo Booth pictures from the event, my mother had apparently turned her rehearsal dinner to Sean at the Sheraton into a "liberation party," as Sean had started taking out his anger towards me onto her behind closed doors, and my mother realizing that for all the toxicity I was spewing, the intent behind it was true. Sean really was only there for the opportunity to cash in on my sister's death settlement.

My mom had moved to the Caribbean in Antigua, where, upon my graduation from probation, we had taken a church carnival cruise with Liberty Tabernacle alumni.

Now, lo and behold, we were accepted into the snooty, upper echelon of church society.

All we had to do was suffer a catastrophic loss to our hearts to now be those at church who could afford such a lavish vacation. That grim knowledge, even on the lavish church cruise, pushed me into blaming God but also vowing not to become as hypocritical and elitist as them and to never forget my humble beginnings as they had. Yet even on that ship, with my devoutly conservative grandmother in tow with us, I was still partying hard and drinking to excess and delirium. I had abandoned Christ completely. I hated Him. Mostly, I hated myself.

I even got in touch with my old trickster friend Sonya, knowing that her shady ways would be a fast track to the party life. So, I started smoking weed with her and binge drinking almost daily while at my boarding house. Sonya was now fifteen but was shocked that I, at nineteen, was still a virgin, and she kept prodding me to give it up. As a young and naive girl trying to fit in, I used my settlement cash to help buy booze. The danger of me using my hard-earned blessings (even for others who use their ill-gotten gains if that's how they gain their money) is that unsavory-minded people of the world will never truly appreciate it.

One such night proved this when, at a random kid's house party, after I had shakingly gone to the ATM and gotten cash out for myself and some to share with them, I indulged in the cheap beer. I wanted to feel something other than miserable. Even though my boarding house caretakers warned me, "You can't drink with these Trazodone pills; it will be very bad if you do." I didn't listen. I was young and fearless; I could take it. I foolishly lied to myself.

After downing three cans, the room started to blur, and I felt a heavy, oppressive slumber come over me like an invisible giant was forcing me to lie on the ground.

I woke hours later, still at the other girl's house, with Sonya dousing me with a cold rag on my head, shouting, "Shut up! She's not a light-weight; she's just not used to this!"

A boy who had been sizing me up since I arrived scoffed in the background. "Yeah, right, she's the oldest one here, and she can't even handle beer," he said, followed by uproarious laughter.

Another girl added, "Yeah, Sonya, you can't bring her back here; look what she did to my carpet. Wow, haha, she really peed herself, dude; what the hell! And she's been foaming at the mouth. Her eyes rolled back in her head. If she's dead or something, man."

Sonya quickly interjected, "She's not dead! Her heart's beating really fast! She's just…"

Finally, it was like my tongue would barely let me force out the words, "No. It's my med. Med-diss-innn."

It was all I could do to force that out.

The next thing I felt was being pushed into the back of Sonya's mom's car, but she wasn't coming with me.

"It's okay, bookey. You are gonna get better."

"Y-You're not coming?" I stammered in terror and pain. But I saw the boy shaking his head and pulling her away and saw others sparking joints and knew that I had killed my chances at gaining any kind of cool points.

In the bright white lights of the hospital, a nurse brought me warm blankets because I was shaking uncontrollably. Practically convulsing.

"Oh, hi, honey. You're awake again. We did some blood work and found high levels of Trazodone in your system. Anything heavier will take a few days to come back. Did you take anything other than what your health chart said, dear?" she asked in a sweet tone, glancing at her clipboard.

At that moment, I panicked, realizing I didn't have my purse or house keys. She handed them to me in a clear bag and I saw that all $400 dollars had been taken, and my debit card. I just knew it was that boy and probably the whole group. I knew I'd have to cancel it before they racked up any huge debt. The nurse insisted I do a rape kit before I left, even though I knew that my wetness was from the anxiety disorder and not an assault. I called a cab and went home to the peaceful boarding house and never spoke of it to anyone.

The sweet caretakers at the boarding home were trained to take care of high-functional adults and acted as my surrogate mothers, giving me home-cooked meals, supportive "baby girl" pet names, and much-needed motherly hugs.

Their words of encouragement when I confided in them about how I was doing did help me immensely. Even still, their gentle concern was no match to the enflamed self-destructive whirlwind path I was on. I was hell-bent on defying God and desecrating my mother's name. Ignoring the fact that I was also desecrating myself.

As I saved money for my first apartment, I started secretly dancing in a strip club called Dreamers. Partially for the money but more for the deviant thrill. Plus, the $1000 a month I was getting from my settlement and hurried furniture spree was not enough to keep my bills paid. I wasn't taught money management amid my mother's blatant abandonment, so I had little to no preparation for the adult world.

It was at these breaking points that I would cry out to God and feel a tinge of His Holy Spirit return to me. I knew I could always come back. But I also knew that I couldn't rest on that prodigal daughter plan forever.

In the years following my first year at Kent State, I learned that both my mother and John had used my social security number to get phones and apartments in my name. Abandoned, scared, and alone, my credit was so low at eighteen that I didn't even qualify for a Verizon cellphone, much to my horror and disbelief. I couldn't understand why until one fateful day, on the way home from classes at Kent, I got an angry call from a bill collector.

The caller was shouting, "We have made several attempts and have found this number from an internal search. You have completely defrauded your account for the yacht payments. You can't deny this is you. We have your social security number linked directly to this account."

"What!" I exclaimed in disbelief. "I'm only nineteen; I could never afford a yacht. What are you talking about?"

The bill collector got silent and then put me on hold. She came back and said, "You said you're nineteen? Oh, that can't be right. We have your date of birth here as 1967. I apologize, ma'am. I think you've had identity theft."

I had to find a Lexington Law firm to challenge fraudulent charges under my social security number.

As I entered Kent State in an Oldsmobile Alero coup I bought for $1000 with a new online boyfriend I met, Zack, a hard rocker type who later I learned saw me crying in court on the front page of the Akron Beacon Journal, I had delved into a life.

CHAPTER 43:

College & Family/Friend Issues...

Due to a falling out at Kent State with a friend and my cousin Layla's instigating involvement, I was now at the University of Akron and not knowing anyone, thrust onto me as her guardian because she had begun partying recklessly, still not as hard as me unbeknownst to her.

Freshman year, I was enrolled at Kent State, I met a girl named Taylor. She was a girl in my history class studying nursing; I am still in fashion. Anyway, she was flunking the course, so I agreed to tutor her in exchange for access to private weed parties and dorm room life. Plus, getting to stay on campus instead of constantly driving back and forth was helping my budget.

It all came to a conclusion one night when I was supposed to go to Taylor's party, but Layla had just moved into the dorms in Akron and basically wouldn't accept that I wouldn't go. She was already calling my aunt Ella to tell her how I wasn't chaperoning her, so I relented. Anyway, Taylor and her friend came to Layla's dorm and had words with me for skipping out on her party because I had just turned twenty-one and could buy liquor.

Despite heavy drinking and partying, I was still managing to get good grades, even getting invited to the National Society of Collegiate Scholars for my merit roll grades.

My cousin Layla, on the other hand, was flunking out completely. Squandering Aunt Ella's hard-earned basketball coaching scholarship in the process.

And out of jealousy and spite at my somewhat underwhelming appearance at Dani's lingerie birthday party I was invited to at the last minute, she would later send me some extremely cruel text messages, effectively ending our cousin bond.

College life continued.

The Taylor girl from history class I had been tutoring was now enraged that I didn't buy her alcohol or go to her KSU party and, instead, sided with my cousin. When it came time for me to retrieve my Victoria's Secret pink duffel bag, outfits, and perfume I had left over, Taylor and her friend from Columbia station started attacking me over the bag.

I remember us both even playing tug-of-war over it, and later, her RA or dorm room leader came rushing in the door exclaiming, "*Two girls on one, like, are you serious? You have to press charges, Jordan.*" This later resulted in her dorm room RA having me press charges as she saw I was alone against the two girls. I chose to resign and enroll in UA even though I wasn't expelled.

Kent State was ruined for me. And my mother's zombie-like state and not at least pleading for me to stop made me move out of her Firestone Park home. On my own. Even though I didn't win the ambush fight, I smiled darkly at the knowledge that in the overly competitive profession of nursing, especially as a KSU alum, you can't even have much of a traffic offense record without being stripped of your title.

Which I didn't want to, but the girl was already calling in the campus police.

Later in court, as a stipulation for getting our charges reduced from, I guess, disorderly conduct to some low-level misdemeanor.

We had to do community service at the Haven of Rest separately, so I met a girl named Lauren who was already at Kent State and was still living in a Twin Lakes-like world that I had come from before, but without the foster care, we seemed to instantly relate to one another.

But unlike me, she was also extremely rebellious, much to my surprise, and we ended up bonding over being the only two girls our age there.

CHAPTER 44:

College, Family Drama, and Nightlife

Also, I realized that we even went to similar schools and liked similar parties. Primo'z in downtown Akron was the spot to be for college kids, and Layla's and Lauren's cliques were there. I remember Lauren just kind of looking uncomfortable because even as a pretty-faced brunette, she still felt out of place.

Primo's was a new hip-hop club, and there were a lot of people dressed to the nines. Some boys were lighting fireworks in the parking lot and, at one point, torched a cop car before they got shut down. I wasn't there for that, but anyway.

The nightclub had opened, and the line wrapped around the block to get in. Our entourage of dorm girls was always rushed in. I was even picked up in the air on the dance floor by this tall and strapping bouncer with dreadlocks.

Layla's clique began dancing beside me, and she enviously retorted, "Oh, so you're the life of the party, huh?" as dancers noticed the skilled moves I'd learned from belly dancing, my special little secret.

"Ha, I guess so. I mean, pretty much!" I called back.

Layla's friend had small bottles of Patron and Hennessy in her friend's car, and we'd pregame in the parking lot, mosh pit type dance, then end up at McDonald's. Layla, always in her sparkly booty shorts, would be the highlight of the night. We have some great photos of us getting ready in my apartment off campus.

We even hit this house party in Akron and started to hang with the crowd, but it was dark and crowded, so we migrated to the porch. We saw a boy, a part of a popular local rap group called G. M. E., pull out a pistol near Layla's car parallel parked right in front of the house and pistol-whipped a boy in the middle of the street. The crowd scattered in shock as We darted for the car, with Layla's new footballer boy toy and friend in tow with us in the backseat. However, she idled by just briefly to catch a quick glance at his silver pistol brandishing under the streetlight, just to show him she showed no fear and then peeled off. Behind us, I turned around, and we heard the trigger pop. I was screaming hysterically for Layla to drive, mad that I let her drive us, and just overprotective and not in a partier's state of mind.

Next for me was Lauren's house party. Lauren had a party at her big suburban house, and I remember I was telling Lauren that I couldn't have vodka, which for Lauren she had been secretly drinking since she was like twelve, so she couldn't really understand. She was nineteen, thinking my twenty-one-year-old fussing was just me being a scaredy cat. She didn't know that when I was in foster care, all of the different medications I was forced to take, and even at twenty-one, were still affecting me from when I was seventeen. Anyway, she, I guess, thought she was being smart and made Jell-O shots with vodka in them with me for her party as her clique, now new familiar faces, started to pour in.

There was a biracial gay boy dancing in her basement by himself, and I naturally love dancing, so I joined him, giggling and getting dizzy with the strobe lights.

Lauren's friends never really danced, not at the nightclub, not at their home party. She was trying to hook me up with this attractive cop blonde boy, but I started getting deathly ill because she made Jell-O shots and put vodka in them with her other friends that she knew longer while I was dancing. They were kind of giggling and telling me that it wasn't vodka. It was the other liquor I had bought, which was some dark liquor.

While Lauren and I and her other friends were placing chips and snacks in bowls, waiting for the boys to arrive, one of Lauren's friends came in gushing, saying, "Oh my God. Like, yeah, so, anyway, when I was in LA the other week I just got back. I have the greatest tan, like wow, y'all are pale, ha-ha."

Lauren and her very blonde friend Ashley kind of scoffed, and the girl went on. "Ha, yeah, my sister lives there and has like a whole house in Beverly Hills. We met Tyga downtown, and my girls and I wanted to hang out with him. He was telling us that his baby's mom, Blac Chyna, was still there and had her stuff in his house. And like wouldn't get out. Like, get out; he doesn't even like you, haha. So, we had to help Tyga move out her stuff, and we would kick some of it down the stairs, hahaha." She laughed haughtily, and the other girls face approving smirks.

I just remember being there in shock that I was really rubbing shoulders with people who knew the celebrity people as regular people. Started also feeling upset, just like this wasn't a place for me. Like how they were all rooting against someone who looks like me in favor of someone who doesn't, like this Kardashian-type girl.

Later, after I got sick from the Jell-O shots, I, of course, started feeling dizzy and sick as the group had gone back down to the basement, and I was upstairs. I tried to go to their patio door as I felt the sickness creeping up, but there was this golden retriever that was snarling at me through their patio in the snow. Eventually, I couldn't take it. I opened it anyway and stood outside. The dog came to sniff my hand and kind of leaped back as I wretched.

Nothing came out, and I felt that maybe the nausea had passed.

Oh, there's like a bunch of deck and patio furniture out here. I really don't want to puke out here, ugh. Maybe I can just make it to the bathroom, I thought to myself as I was going back. I was by the corner of the couch on the carpet; a slight stumble sent it all crashing out.

When they came back in, I had furiously scooped up most of it into grocery bags from the store, and it was just the actual stain, not the sopping mess.

I remember the cop boy just kind of staring at me in shock.

I drove home with the Jell-O shot that was wiped off with some swipes of paper towels, trying to spray perfume on me, crying, and praying to God grumblingly.

I remember I had my Oldsmobile Alero coupe driving in the snow, and I actually drove into a ditch, but I drove myself out of it on the way home.

But later, as I was finishing the Haven of Rest thing with Lauren, our friendship did have a chance to recover from that. It was actually a different issue that ended our friendship.

She was understandably mad at me for the mess and told me I could've stayed and helped, but there was nothing else I could do. On the phone, I told her, "I cleaned up as much as I could in, and I told you I was allergic to vodka in the first place, but you still gave me those shots!" And clicked the phone.

After seeing Lauren at the Haven of Rest for work, we decided to go out to Primo's another time with her click and then go to Taco Bell afterward. Layla's clique wasn't there, and neither was Tyga's LA fling girl, so I was really the only girl who could guide them through the hip-hop world. I remember the same cute bouncer guy that had picked me up before picked me up again, and we danced like that sensually in the air for a minute, as Lauren's clique cheered for me. I really was the life of the party that night; it was a blast!

My feisty cousin Layla wasn't there to compete with my shine, and the other girls just weren't ready to be as hungry as my family was, so in that moment, I redeemed myself, and we had a good night. Until Lauren's jealousy started to creep in, but it wasn't based on a sexual type of jealousy, but our deeper beliefs and political issues that we knew were going to always be prevalent eventually.

So, our falling out was over political differences when I was at her house one time watching a movie with her, and we were showing pictures of her ex-boyfriend. An Obama presidential ad came on, as he was running for president at the time, and her parents were sweethearts but still conservative and on the fence about who to vote for.

Anyway, it was nice that Lauren had enough character. Let something like a serious belief, rather than a petty mishap, end our rocky-built friendship.

End of Relationship with Cousins

"**A**nyways. Come on, photoshoot time!" I squealed and stood in front of her balloons and streamers. Her party was lavishly done, with rose petals on the beds and floors, LED lights for photo ops, jewel-encrusted Hennessy bottles, and strawberry champagne lining the counters. I arrived in my black fur-trimmed trench coat I had gotten from my time working at T.J.Maxx. We hugged, and I still felt that tinge of cousin love return to us. She thought I looked kind of cute, but I exclaimed, "I only had two hours, yo late self!" And she let out a shy giggle and then guided me towards the bathroom, where risqué shower photos were being taken.

She even photographed me, saying, "Dang, Miss New Booty!"

I couldn't help but start giggling in the shower, feeling like Marilyn Monroe doing my burlesque-style poses while she directed me.

I still have mad love for that girl despite the family drama trying to divide us.

"Okay. Photoshoot time, y'all! Come on!" I shouted and gathered her and her birthday twin, Ingrid, under the pink balloons and glittery streamers.

Our photo turned out cute. I made a schmoozing lip pose and arched my foot; she arched hers towards me, and Ingrid let out the first posh smile she had cracked all night. It wasn't exactly sexy like the theme, but it was cute how I wanted.

She shared the birthday hotel party with her best friend, Ingrid. They called themselves ebony and ivory because Dani's biracial. Sharon had a fling from big Antwan with an Italian boy before she had Tariq and Adrian.

Layla, in a red Lacey leotard, looked gorgeous next to Dani's black lace leotard with a fur-trimmed silk robe. She sparked a joint in the adjacent hotel room and looked unimpressed with my outfit.

I hurriedly said, "Layla! Ah, girl, you look so beautiful! Model like always!"

To which all she replied was a simple, "Huh. Thanks." Her phone flashed with a notification, and she swiped it while I was reaching for a hug.

I nodded, and since she wasn't filling the silence, I continued, "Oh my God, it's been like two years since we last saw each other on campus, right? I know I'm late, but aye, at least I still made it! Haha."

But Layla just stared at me for a long time, then nodded and muttered, "Yeah," while puffing her blunt. Her phone flashed again, and she opened it while I was talking.

The joint was being passed around to some boys behind her, and she started talking to them while I was trying to catch up with her. Then I finally asked, "Um, hello, aren't you gonna pass it to me?"

She stared at me again for a long time, then muttered, "Ha, yeah, girl. Here you go." And walked out.

I walked to the mirror and realized my makeup was melting from the steam in the shower, and Layla hadn't even told me.

I didn't understand where her cold sullenness was coming from. I was trying so hard to make up for lost time, trying to heal after Faith's shocking murder, becoming so busy with work and school, and yet, my family was still my family. I decided that even after several shots of Hennessy, I still drove back from Youngstown to Akron so I wouldn't miss class in the morning. Dani was nervous but hugged me and gave me her blessing. She really did try her best, but she had had a secret wedding with her high school sweetheart and had two small kids I was getting to know, so I understood it.

My aunt organized family photos at Olan Mills, which I'm still glad that I soldiered on and bit my tongue to do. Because family, good or bad, is really all you have. And I wanted my cousins to see how much I was fighting for life, not to succumb to despair, and to have something positive to look back on at me even if we wouldn't stay together forever.

I finally realized where Layla's harshness was coming from. I thought it over about her hysterical model scout phone call. Her story about her car. Dropped her off by Garfield Heights and realized the dealership was closed. More notably, in very close proximity to where I had dropped Antwan off in Garfield Heights. I was so busy with college at the University of Akron that I couldn't notice that my cousin was being influenced by Antwan to revive the old family beef from when our parents would fall out, forcing us to take a side in childhood. I somewhat understood where Layla's and Antwan's harshness was coming from, but not fully yet.

A few weeks later, I started getting texts from Layla sending me some unflattering candid photos she had caught of me secretly on her new iPhone with a text saying, "The wrong twin died, you fake, fat B word."

Partially, I think it was out of jealousy for flunking out of the University of Akron. Partially because she was caught in between more drama on the Homefront.

During a home visit, after all of the buildup of Layla's college had worn off, a family friend, Makai, started to heckle and expose her in Aunt Ella's kitchen, saying, "Shut yo dumb self up; that's why you flunked out college. Ahh. Haha. Lame. She a clown, family!"

I saw Layla's face flush red, and I waited in silence for a clever, snappy comment, but she just stood there in silence. She just froze, almost like she was even imitating my noticeable moment of silence during Antwan's taunts at me.

I finally understood where my cousin Layla's harshness was coming from.

Stunned by the sudden attack, I logged on to Facebook to see more comments underneath photos of me with church friends saying, "Don't believe the hype; she doesn't look like this. She edits her pictures."

I tried appealing to Dani about it with a screenshot, but time had passed, and she had begun a wildly popular makeup business out of her home, so she wasn't having it. She blocked me, and Layla shortly after. Heartbroken at my distorted life in comparison to my cousins. Heartbroken at the tragedy setting me back so far from my true potential, and it not being anyone's fault.

I knew then that I was forcing the family connection and wearing myself out in the process, while getting little to no amounts of effort in return, and I vowed to give up on my extended family once and for all.

CHAPTER 46:

Returning Back to Christ, a Prodigal Daughter

Eventually, I decided that I had had my fill of rebelling against God because overdosing on Trazodone, keeping up a rigorous exercise routine to stay in shape for my secret club job while still chasing this collegiate career, that pursuit in itself starting to feel like I was playing a game. A tortuous, never-ending game of trying to catch an unobtainable flag. But the thought of quietly disappearing from the academic world after I had professors critiquing my best work. Going into debt just to quietly disappear from college like a lot of my acquaintances did, at times, felt so tempting. But the thought also enraged me to think about actually living out.

I decided that the secret dance life would have to go. I'd have to give up that connection to impulsive, wild nightlife fully and go back to God. I always felt like my life was most productive when I had a connection to God again. Even the occasional church visits seemed to be restoring my youth. These conclusions led me to really be real with myself and admit to myself that life without the Holy Spirit was a hundred times worse. Just emptiness and tension and mistrust. I don't know how it works for others who make the party work seem all so wonderful, but it clearly wasn't like that for me.

CHAPTER 47:

Trying to Move On with Mom

Still, some notable exceptions to my mother's mid-life crisis happened before we completely lost touch. In 2012, my mother organized a trip to Israel for us. Saying it was an homage to our beautiful Faith. We got to see the holy sites. Even Jesus' tombstone and gurney in Jerusalem. We stayed for about two weeks before we flew back to the Caribbean. The first half of the year was lush on the white sandy beaches, hum of seagulls and soft reggae, and swarthy-skinned men to serve you coconut rum on the beach at your leisure. As an avid swimmer, even teaching Faith how to swim as early as eleven, after a quick impromptu lesson I'd given her, teaching her how to float on her back, hands underneath her back, resting on the waves as I let her go, one summer night at a beach in Niles. A lifetime ago, it felt like nineteen-year-old me enjoyed the picturesque school of fish colorfully swimming underneath me. A much-needed respite before and the nightmare of my mother's mental and physical health loomed like a dark cloud over our beach.

I think my constant partying had momentarily shocked my mother into being that mother I once had in the suburbs of Twin Lakes. The mother who read me Shakespeare plays and taught me about black heroes in history like the Amistad slave ship revolt. Taught me to love my culture. And to find the honor in suffering for a noble cause.

Even still, in Israel, I was still mad at God. But a part of that little girl I once was before the storm of Faith's murder hit re-emerged.

CHAPTER 48:

Tel Aviv, Israel. Serious Come-to-Jesus Moment

Even in Israel, after the church cruise, I was still in my rebellious ways. Nothing seemed to erase the pain of losing my twin sister or make me want to try to keep on living. I was hell-bent on giving up on God, period. Yet, on our tour through Jerusalem, I noticed I was getting several catcalls from Muslim boys and couldn't help but get enraptured with this amazing experience. They were acting like I was a celebrity. I couldn't understand it until my mother explained that people on this side of the world rarely see African American people other than on TV. The closest they see are the Egyptian and Haitian Africans, whose beautiful swarthy skin seemed to almost glisten and definitely showed me how different Americanized black people are from them.

Still, I was in awe. And reveling in the beauty of Israel, soaking up the star treatments as we passed shop after shop, some shop owners had old, crinkled pictures of Beyoncé and started shouting out to me as if I was her. Again, still in my rebellion against God, I vowed to myself not to let myself fully open my heart to seeing the holy sites.

In retrospect, I regret not taking the opportunity to adorn myself in elegant attire to match the prominence of this ancient piece of world history. Yet I did not. And this is my testimony. Raw and exposed. Like an exposed nerve. An unabashed look into what most Christians cover with a vague "I've been there" or a "I had my wild times" while never seeming remotely like someone who had lived in the twenty-first century.

And un-sugarcoated glossing over the true depth of my anger at God.

While my mother pulled out her purple leather jacket with a fur trim and I saw others dressed ornately, I chose a brightly colored hoody covered in stars that I had resigned were representing the star of David and a fur trim to somewhat match my mother's style. But mainly to show how anarchist I was toward God, Christ, and life, period.

Anyway, I think the Holy Spirit taught me a very hard lesson for that blatant disregard for such a sacred dwelling, which manifested in a blazingly real way. As I was leaving the church of the holy sepulcher after seeing Jesus' gurney, the very same gurney that was used to cart his body off after His crucifixion, I ran my fingers down the jagged wooden planks, still stained with strewn, dark blood streaks, to this present day as of 2012. I was in awe as I stared at the billowing silver incense candle holders, steadily churning out gorgeous smelling and colorful frankincense and myrrh clouds of scent.

After my mother and I took turns taking photos, we then entered the tombstone, seeing it encrusted in red rubies that were being warmed underneath candles on an alabaster-looking platform, giving off an ominous glow. We emerged outside. Just in time to see a long line of monks had begun congregating and swayed their own gongs of frankincense and myrrh while singing impassioned prayers that almost sounded like battalion chants, all against the uproarious bell tower sounds, signaling noon.

A streak of some glittering sun broke through the cloudy day sky momentarily, and I got a majestic shot of a tapestry waving against the wailing wall-like side of the cathedral.

The glint from the sun showed a sparkling ray of sunshine just as the clouds started to roll back over. When I lowered my camera, there stood another tall, handsome Muslim man outside, smiling at me as if he were waiting for me.

"You are quite beautiful. What brings you to this historic place?" He asked inquisitively. He then offered me lunch at a cafe he owned to learn more about me.

I excitedly agreed and ran over to my mom to give her my digital camera.

"He says he can make me a frappe Israel, er, I mean, Muslim style."

My mom questioned me for several moments, and I grew anxious that this strapping guy would get away.

After my consistent prodding, she relented and sighed to an Asian girl from our tour she'd been chatting with. "My daughter. Forgive her; she's hopelessly American," my mom said to the gentle laughter of our tour, who I noticed were all covertly spread out, looking in various directions, yet idling in close proximity to each other and fearless, mountain climbing, war veteran tour guide.

He was busy narratively explaining some history of the ancient artifacts around us. I darted back to mystery man, whose smile briefly looked like a grim flat line, and then he hurriedly said, "Here, it's only around the corner. Come, my love," while ushering me along.

I yelled another quick reply to my mom that I'd be right across the street, and be right back, then off we went on our adventure. The tour guide had warned us not to get lost while on our holy guide tour because the Muslims still prey on tourists and brag about owning many of the sights found in the Bible through years of war and conquer. Some shouts I heard as we walked were, "This is not Jesus's land; this is now *our* land!" and "What god would lose ownership of His own temples?" were being shouted to our tour as we ascended up the steep cobblestone streets.

Still, I persisted. It was about five minutes into the walk when I said, "This is far enough. You said it was right next door. What is this?"

"No, no, beautiful. Come, it is just right here. Please sit," he said and pulled out a brassy and curly-cued style chair for me. A waiter brought him tea and coffee for me, and I started to feel very cosmopolitan as some stares and whispers came our way. Yet I was disappointed that he didn't really have a frappuccino like he had smiled and said yes, of course, to when I'd asked.

It wasn't like a Starbucks, though; it was steaming hot and bitter, but after some rather insistent protest, he snapped and hissed at his waiter to bring me some cream.

"Ah. Yes. He is my nephew," he said and smiled as the guy tossed two cream packets by the kettle and shot him a gilded smirk. I sipped the coffee and listened as he kept showering me with compliments. "You are beautiful enough to be my wife. Like today," he said, chuckling. "I even own the building above me. You should stay here with me."

At that moment, I got a wave of terror and heard my mother scream my name in a blood-curdling shout. "Jordan! Jordan!" she wailed. "Oh, Jordan Noelle Fin. Lee!" she screamed with her head tilted to the sky.

I caught a glimpse of her mauve purple leather jacket and yelled, "Marmee, where are you?"

"Just follow my voice. Hurry, the tour guide said we have to go," she cried back.

I could just make out the tour herding her back through the sea of people. But I was lost. I tried not to panic and record some views with my camcorder. But I started feeling dizzy and foggy.

I tried to act like I wasn't lost as I was going through the seas of people. I thought of something I could do quickly that would look like I knew what I was doing, so I grabbed my purse and went in to look for my debit card. I patted and didn't feel anything but my make up bag and felt my heart sink. I started panting as I realized I didn't have my passport or even my ID.

Just then, a boy holding a large brass instrument came over to me and said, "You. Yes, you. Come, come. I have some expensive jewels. They will look beautiful on you. Come, it's okay."

The light drizzle rain from earlier was picking up again and coming down hard and fast, and crowds of people were swarming to get underneath awnings of buildings for cover.

I started to walk towards the merchant, then quickly darted away when his back was turned into the crowds of people moving me to and fro.

Men running to cover carts with tarps, babies crying in bassinets, girls and teens dashing into stores, wiping rain from their faces, and the smells of different foods swirling all around me in the air.

As I was walking against the awnings, I was getting soaked. My jacket and jeans were sticking to me as people whizzed by me in a blur.

I even leaned on the side of a building and prayed briefly before gathering myself and moving on.

After about an hour of trying to appear as if I hadn't lost my tour, the even more unsavory thought came that the scalding cup of coffee could've even been the cause of my rapid health decline. But I was away from that predatory guy, thank God. The immediate threat of being trapped in Israel, without even my debit card, was my most immediate issue. My mom had insisted on carrying my debit card and passport while we were touring the ancient cities. Back in the posh capital, Tel Aviv, when it came time to go shopping in their Times Square-esque skyscraper malls, after being wanded with metal detectors to get in. My mom scoffed lightly at my disheveled expression.

"You do realize that these Muslims have thrown grenades into Israeli school buses back in the 90s at Gaza Strip, right?" And those newsreels talking about insurgent wars in the Middle East briefly came back to me. It was there she'd let me have my wallet, but never before that.

I continued recording as my occasional asks for help were drawing suspicious eyes and other Muslim boys selling colorful tapestries and brass instruments came approaching me, trying to beckon me to talk.

The rain patted down hard pats fiercely, clearing the streets for several minutes while people looked for spaces to duck under. As I was being jostled in the close-quartered village, I lost my camcorder, but thankfully, my mother still had our digital camera. The rain picked up and my jacket was completely drenched, barely being able to find a space under a tent, with some women shop owners shooing me away if I did not immediately purchase something.

It was then that I was startled and tapped by an Irish couple who was on the tour with us. "Oh my God, there you are!" they exclaimed. "Your mother has been beside herself screaming; we even skipped a stop on the tour because she wouldn't let the tour guide go until you were found."

The tour guide man, a muscular man even in his sixties, said, "You're lucky your mother cares about you so much. There have been many girls who go with that man who don't come back again."

"Many girls go with that man? Why have you not reported him?" a man from our tour exclaimed.

The tour guide smiled a wry and world-weary smile and said calmly but firmly, "We have. For years. They just keep reopening under different names. You are a very fortunate girl that you have the mother you do." For the first time since Faith's murder, I started to believe the same.

Later, I got to visit the Yad Vashem Holocaust Museum. Yad Vashem means *remember the names* in Hebrew. A day or so later, I became deathly ill. A home-visiting doctor told me I had caught a virus that was going around. Later, the correlation between that free offer of coffee on my tour stop at Jesus' crucifix gurney sunk in for me.

CHAPTER 49

Reclaiming My Birth Right in Christ

Fighting the odds against me. Being a first-generation college student. And accepting that my mother didn't have the will to do the same.

The trip to Israel somewhat restored our mother-daughter bond, and probation ended for good for that false charge. I had decided to step out on Faith and join my mother on her journey of reinventing herself. We flew back to the Caribbean, and the peace lasted for a bit. We had candlelit beach dinners, and I snorkeled during the days. Yet, the threat of instability turning back into a nightmare loomed. Later, I realized my mother's soul-searching journey was actually more of a mid-life crisis. Anyway, it took about six months in Antigua with my mom before things became crazy again.

She was back to being impulsive in dating. After two dates, she gloated to me like a schoolgirl about handsome prison warden Deon, a part-time reggae singing at the popular Sandal's beach resort, Dickinson's Bay. According to my mom's new assistant, Darren, who had taken to running errands for my mom, driving her old Jeep at times, taking our Yorkie twin puppies Cindy and Toby to be groomed, buying groceries, even cashing her checks much to my dismay and scolding, Deon serenaded my mother in a sombrero in front of the tiki coconut rum bar and then to an all-white beach party by night. Darren also had an on-again, off-again girlfriend, whose name escapes me, but they met somewhere in the Town Square shopping center and happened to have twin daughters, two tall and gangly eleven-year-olds named Jekayla and Shekayla.

My mom kept insisting that Faith and I looked identical to them, and upon meeting prison warden Deon once, he was slowly coming onto me while my mother pretended to ignore it, quickly changing the topic to her latest jewel-encrusted ring needing to be cleaned, or to the money they could make with a car rental service on the small island, that currently had only one car service.

I started worrying as Deon casually mentioned that I'd be calling him "daddy" soon if my mom kept loving him this good. My worry grew. Yet my persistent pleas for my mother to expel exactly which bills were set on automatic payment, comparing prices of villas she'd move us to every couple of months or so, began to be met with more and more aggression from her.

"When you get three men to put a ring on your finger, not just sleep with you, then tell me about life, missy," she quipped and even recruited some of her entourage to join in some dutiful snickers.

Slowly but surely, she started controlling me again as if I was still that shy, homeschooled girl at her mercy. Going as far as to revoke my debit card at the drop of a hat. She said she did it to protect me, which I knew was partially true, but really, she completely disregarded each protest I made to keep up with her lavish lifestyle.

After my throat ulcer extraction surgery, my own mother's grief started manifesting in a physical health issue; she started having hot flashes and would come home only after a short errand pouring sweat. Even having a high blood pressure monitor administered to her person, as she had started fainting at random on days that she'd stranded me at home to go to museums and shops.

One night, I cornered her when she came and demanded a flight back home while she was playing on her iPad one night. Physically watched her book the flight, and she grudgingly agreed, but only with my debit card number, though. On my connecting flight from Puerto Rico to Florida, I realized my mother had booked a flight for me that had left the previous day before I arrived. It cost the money I'd need for a cab ride home from the airport to book a hotel, and I rebooked a flight by over-drafting my account before it was completely in the negative and would go through.

Still, I flew back to our home in Firestone Park. Lived without water out of an old water jug for almost a month as I discovered that my mom had lied and stopped paying the bills altogether there; even still, by the grace of God, a few showers at Allie's and Jill's, I made it to orientation for freshman year at Kent, and with my new laid back rocker boyfriend Zack's help was starting to find myself out of the despair.

Then, one day, to my heart-dropping shock, my mother showed up. A despondent, disheveled shell of herself. No glittering crazy long polished nails, long glossy weaves, perfectly applied makeup, or expensive QVC outfits. My mother was in grey sweats and had lost at least thirty pounds.

Her latest fiancé project, the drill sergeant prison guard Deon, obviously more attracted to my mother's lavish spending than to her, actually ended up arresting her out of spite during one of their fights for her not following through on a car rental business she had promised to upstart with him.

She told me, "I know, spending those few odd months in that Caribbean jail, that Caribbean hell hole." She sighed deeply, looking at the porch the whole time. "I know it was God punishing me for having you sent to jail for no good reason. I see why you left me. Look at you. Still trying to get an education when I failed you. There were live rats in that jail. I had to sleep on a cot. Only a bucket for a bathroom. I…" she trailed off. "I failed you. And I don't think I'll ever be your mother again. I lied to you, too. And for all the good it did me. You know Sean stole $40,000 from me when I called off our wedding the night before? It was because you were right. He told me after the wedding that the days of me talking back were over. And I saw John's face in his and fled."

"Can't you sue him?" I countered.

"No!" my mother roared. "Stop it. The day Children Services came, they weren't going to take you. I told them to. I told them to let you be molested by some racist foster parents since my doing back-breaking work while you two complained about being homeschooled wasn't good enough for you. And I don't deserve you as a daughter."

"Mommy, please stop," I said. "I had been in contact with Jill and even in the midst of my own toxic ways, Jill was still being a rock for me. I had started paying her rent while I fought to upkeep the house she let go to hell. God is still with us. And I'm not gonna give up. I'm gonna keep going to college until I graduate and make something of myself for you and Faithy."

As of 2022, I can finally say that thanks to God, I am now a college graduate. A first-generation one at that. Yet the years following that metamorphosis out of darkness and back into God's loving arms, I saw my mother's mental health slip away from me, unfortunately, never to return again.

For a while, I took care of my mom as she had stopped speaking since she had come back home from that prison in Antigua. Even still, I soldiered on. I was going to make something of myself for my slain sister's sake. Even if my mother wouldn't. I would go back to church sometimes back at Liberty Tabernacle, but the church politics would drive me back into the party scene.

My mother, sensing that I had gone back to dancing occasionally, had decided one night after I had finished classes at Kent and was coming home from my new job at a massage parlor instead of the club to show me how much it was hurting her in a terrifying way. From 2013 to 2014, this was the first attempt she had made at taking her own life.

She called me while I was at work and told me in a muffled voice. "I can't breathe. Please call someone. I love you."

In a panic, I dashed home, calling Allie on my drive home. I was met by Jill Flagg, our former lawyer, Allie, and an ambulance team.

I heard Jill saying, "That toxicology report can't be right. Cocaine? Toni would never do cocaine. She does suffer from chronic fatigue and takes tramadol. It's a powerful pain medication, but it shouldn't have caused that kind of reading." Her voice shook. Jill and my mother had grown very close throughout Faith's murder trial. Sharing habeas corpus knowledge in law that only they understood, bonding over in-depth theological talks they'd have late at night. It was in 2013 that we spent Thanksgiving and even Christmas with Jill and her family. My mother made her famous apple cinnamon cheesecake and gourmet dishes. My mom was always an expert chef. I think the scare shocked more than just myself.

Anyway, at the Haven of Rest, I saw Tara again when I was finishing up the community service. We were serving ham and meals to the residents and noticed they even had a shopping area for the patrons. As I was running back and forth to the kitchen, I saw a girl sitting on the linoleum floor with duffel bags and sleeping bags, a small toddler bouncing on her knee, and an African-American man with really long, yet scraggly and unkempt dreadlocks, and in amazement, I realized it was Tara from the Secured Treatment Center.

I rushed over to her at first, then stopped because she looked kind of disheveled; I didn't want to startle her.

I had to exclaim, "Tara! Is that you from way back in the day?"

Her face whipped up, and then when she saw me, she just lit up and said, "Oh my God, Jordan? I never knew what came of you, wow! Like, look at you! You're so beautiful and put together!"

We hugged, and I prayed for her.

Later, on my drive home, I realized just how blessed I still was by God. How much of a blessing it was that even in spite of everything

I went through in foster care, I still had more hope and faith for the future (Jeremiah 29:11) than a girl who had truly been forgotten by the system.

It brought my mind to what is the most important. Not chasing fame but chasing my faith in Christ. Seeing Tara again made me see it through to create Faith Forever ministries, the foster care nonprofit initiative to remind people to count their blessings every day in a fashionable way, too. Hey now!

Life at College, No Fam, Mom. Just Me And God

The last time I saw my mom was in 2016, after the Faith's Kitchen Church Dedication Ceremony. Mark and I had grown apart a lot as I planned the ceremony and tried to tend to my mother's instability, and she told me she was moving out of Ohio for good. I became consumed with my college career at UA and tried to move on from the drama, and I was relieved at the break from my mother's issues.

Yet, as time went on, I would try to stay in touch with her on Facebook. In 2017, I landed a Fashion Week Internship for Paris Fashion Week, for the University of Akron Fashion Abroad Program and got some positive comments from her (when she wasn't randomly sending cryptic messages to me), and I was elated that she got to see that before we officially lost touch.

The next news I got from her was in 2020. I'd moved a lot since the house-buying attempt. Became engaged to Mark in 2015. Mark and I had become somewhat codependent on each other when we met on Plenty of Fish's dating website.

I was reeling from my mother's absentee behavior and trying to forge this new life, this new house, and a new normal outside of the prevalent grieving of losing my twin sister.

Mark was reeling from his own literal war stories from a tour in Iraq and Afghanistan and coming to terms as a newfound Christian himself. He told me stories of growing up in Dayton. He started working in factories as early as eight years old to support his single mom and brothers. The night his dad came to his trailer when he was the same age and shot up the house for about twenty minutes. The fear of hiding in the bathtub with his mother fueled him into fights, but he wanted to channel his rage into something positive. He said he was starting to think it was impossible without God, which I admired. He was especially good-looking, too, resembling a Matt Damon type with a shaved head. I related to his relentless pursuit, from conditioning his body in the gym very young to going to Iraq and Afghanistan shortly after 9/11.

After about seven months of dating, even having him meet Allie, he proposed to me with his Marine Corps "Battle of Iwo Jima" ring. Yet I called it off in 2016 because of his unresolved PTSD. And because of a fateful last visit I got from my mom one night, leaving me this letter she wrote. I still have the photo I took of it, which I'll add in the addendums at the end.

Anyway, my mom had chosen the letter as a form of communication, which I still graciously accepted over the ominous suicide phone call approach. She was growing incensed with the massage parlor job I had picked up to get away from the lure of the fast-money clubs for something safer. The massage parlor was actually a nursing school in North Canton, training STNAs and certifying them as professional masseuses. I worked under her as an apprentice practitioner. Deep tissue massages were performed in a room with a space heater, mood lighting, medical massage table, heated lotion platforms and hot towels were prepared adjacent to the classrooms. A forty-five-minute massage could result in the standard fifty dollars house fee earning, with upwards to a hundred dollars bills being left by the end table as we came in to sterilize the room, didn't seem all that unsavory to me.

My cousin Amber, who I didn't know as well as my other cousins, but again, hopelessly optimistic, without Christ, fighting for the family for the sake of blood relation, or blood being thicker than water, as she called it, I agreed to work at her STNA job for a couple of months. I quit when she tried to coerce me to go further in rubbing a client down with her and bragged to Aunt Ella about having me "pimped out."

At the family reunion in 2017 at Huntington Beach in Cleveland, my relatives were raving about my fashion week internship in Paris, France, and I was able to redeem my name and credibility in my elder's eyes when Amber, having lost custody of all of her children, attempted the expose trend.

She wasn't nearly as good at it as Antionette, however, who left me this reeling letter the last time I heard from her:

Jordan,

The problem we have here is an unwillingness to face the truth. I will just repeat what you yourself had said recently. I guess I do have a problem. I should have listened to you.

The night you cursed me horribly in Walmart for the heinous crime of making a face, I was barely speaking above a whisper when I tried to get you to see you needed help with the economy, and was I raising my voice? No. Was I raising my voice last night? No.

Your demeanor does wear on me. I am, after all, only a human being, so there will be times when I get emotional, just like any other normal person, that in no way "causes" or justifies this continued madness.

If I'm "an instigating jerk," my dear, then what do you say of your actions? Constantly returning to the same tiresome nasty arguments like the copying nonsense about your behavior recently. The hot topic incident this whole business with Amber had nothing to do with me. Are you going to seek help before you destroy yourself or continue to use me as your scapegoat?

*You believe that when you are incensed or angered, you
have the right to do or say anything, whether it's me or
someone else. If you do not face the truth, there are dark days
ahead for you.*

*Unfortunately, being a weak, sinful human, I have abso-
lutely no ability to always do and say things perfectly at all
times. But as a person who knows me intimately, who sees me
doing my utmost to rely on Jesus through my trials and pain,
often minute by minute, you can't really believe that I would
set out to purposely lie to my daughter about anything.*

*Also, I've been quite frank with you about all of the
emotions that have been churning inside me as a result of this
probable pregnancy. I'm glad this incident occurred today for
one reason only: it's crystal clear that you simply should obtain
an abortion; you are in no shape to deal with this any other
way, as far as I can see.*

*Jordie, we need to get you into the PureLife residential
program for intensive, Jesus-centered help. Consider this an
intervention because I simply cannot continue to live in this
madness any longer. If you don't consent to treatment, then we
must part ways. You can keep this house; I'll leave.*

*I want no more hateful vileness between us. I hope you
received this letter in the spirit it was given: heartbroken
sorrow, but most of all, love.*

— Mommy

After the Fashion Week Internship, I came home, and by 2018, I was
somewhat relapsing back into instability. Decided to keep fighting for
my faith in God and my college career. Moved into the depot, the

newly renovated college dormitory in downtown Akron, and joined the Christian youth group Campus Focus, even accompanying them on a Florida mission trip. Then, I got a job at Starbucks at the Student Union, and things were finally starting to look up and feel hopeful.

I finally made it as a junior with fifty credits, which is a huge milestone as each four-month-long class only equates to two to four credits, and that's only if you pass with a higher than a C average.

Then the Coronavirus happened. My chosen plan of going at a snail's pace of only going to school halftime to party and indulge in my double life had finally caught up with me. My major, fashion merchandising, was also being eradicated due to budget cuts. And I was running out of financial aid. Also, getting into fights at college parties wasn't helping my case.

Then, the biggest blow of them all came as the world went into quarantine. I'd received news that my mother was pronounced dead from an overdose of painkillers in Tijuana, Mexico. January 3, 2020.

That's when I realized that the party was over for me. For good.

CHAPTER 51:

Coming to Terms with My Mother's Shocking Death and Finding Myself Out of the Grief with Grit and God

That declaration that the party was over for me literally saw me drop everything.

As a power of attorney over my mother's estate and will, I learned that my mother was found dead in Tijuana, Mexico, due to an overdose of her tramadol rheumatoid pain medication. This wasn't the first scare she had given me, but her disappearance from my life for those five years, 2015 to 2020, would bring a new chapter of clarity and realization of my life and determination to document my life, as now two critical parts of it were no longer on this earth.

I moved out of the fancy depot and back to my first apartments, humble and quaint. I even rode the bus for a year because I was in such shock and pain from my mom's death that I couldn't take the thought of driving. My UA Akron Zips card let me ride free all that year, another silver lining I chose to see as a small blessing from God, letting me know He hadn't forgotten me.

My aunt Ella and uncle Jerry did come to pick me up from the depot in 2020. I tried to think that maybe, maybe, this new tragedy would make us a real family. Yet, back in that kitchen, it was still the same toxicity. Layla lied about sending that ridiculously cruel text and instead bragged about her barber college degree. My aunt had invited a neighbor to start gloating about a boy we had seen at the gas station who she said looked like the R&B singer August Alsina. The neighbor lady let out a hysterical "Girl!" before getting the juicy details.

One thing I learned from all of my various hospital stints was this: the definition of insanity is doing the same thing over and over, expecting a different result to happen.

In the height of my sophomore to junior year at Akron, before I went to Paris, I'd managed to make my mother follow through with her promise to dedicate our home church's kitchen to Faith. Only Layla, Gale, and my cousin Tori showed up to it in 2016. My former Marine fiancé's imposing stature helped coerce my reluctant pastor into following through, and he even uncovered my mother, whom I had banished from my home after she tried overdosing in my new home in Fairlawn. She was in a halfway house after she had run her new Audi off the road, still in her transient mid-life crisis state.

Even despite the chaos, after Faith's dedication ceremony, people began to remember her story. The story of the brave girl who defended her roommate Margaret in a vicious attack, the girl who had the courage to speak up for herself and others. A girl wise beyond her years. Even with her own troubles, being in foster care, little girls messaged me about memories of Faith praying with them when they were scared in the night.

The resurgence of hope and love I had for my crazily courageous twin manifested itself in an upstart nonprofit foundation. I named it Faith Forever Ministries after her and created a website for her in

2016. It took me hours of studying HTML and algorithms, but the discipline of college helped me see it done. I even hosted a fundraiser for the battered women's shelter of Summit County in homage to the time I had spent there, escaping the clutches of my terrifying step-father as a kid. I even had Margaret attend with her four beautiful children, and she wrote a glowing review of her take on the incident that I'll add in after.

That's my "what's next" move. I know that I still have a long way to go in terms of healing. But I'm thankful for those days leading me out of my pursuit of party life and "keeping up with the Jones" mindset. I'm thankful for being brought back into humble living, the days I worked and stood outside in the blistering cold waiting for the hopeful lights and hum of the bus. Even getting free rides all around the city with my now defunct but still issuable UA ID card.

For the grueling long ten-hour shifts at a call center for people with emergency relief benefits directly after COVID-19. The irate customers would make my blood boil, but the few gems I got would tell me how comforting my words were to them. In a stage of life where I felt worthless and hopeless, being motherless and familyless, I found it still wasn't really true.

The despair drove me to cling to Christ in a way I had only dreamed of doing. I started watching Juanita Bynum's sermons and Sarah Jakes Robert's testimonies and even found my voice to sing for the Lord again.

And as if by some miracle, God even rewarded me with being accepted into a job at UA at Barnes and Noble once the school opened back up.

There, I met a sweet and soft-spoken girl named Bella. I could tell she was a freshman and nervous. I could see in her the eyes of adoration one sees in the face of a child who looks up to their older brother, appreciating their strengths and hoping one day to emulate them.

Anyway, through my natural confidence born out of ten years working in retail at malls and posh outlets, I had the courage to ask for her Instagram.

There, I was invited to her sorority party. Only this time, it wasn't a competition of elitist ego or alcohol-fueled college events. The sorority was called Chi Alpha. And it was a Christian sorority. Even in all my rebellion, God still showed me that my efforts to reconcile my heart to Him hadn't gone unnoticed.

By the grace of God, I spent 2021 doing sorority outreach and doing praise parties at a church in Kent State. Only now, I was all too eager to go worship Jesus, even if there were still some snooty side eyes from some Christian mean girls who hadn't yet experienced enough life to realize the beauty in it. I didn't care. I felt so on fire for God in the way I had when I was a young girl, only even more strong than before.

Now, I'm a graduate, and I'm not sure what's next. I'm definitely still going to go for that bachelor's degree. But more importantly, I want the bachelor's degree of Christ's honor anchoring my life now. Through the new storms that may come. Breaking through those dark, muddy clouds into a sunny silver lining. I want God there with me. Even though He always was. Now, I want Him there directing my sails, as well as being my distress call during rainy days.

I don't know where I'm going 100 percent of the time. But I want Him. I choose Christ. And I thank Him for letting me see the highs and lows of life to know intrinsically just how precious the gift of Christ's love truly is. And I hope my candor may inspire someone else to break out of their shell and embrace God in the same way they pursue fleeting pleasures. Because there's nothing like the name of Jesus, y'all. Truly, nobody is like Him.

These memories are so precious, and I'm glad that even on hard days, you can always read a page of your memories in photos and step right back into that happy place. That grateful place. Because so many others don't have that blessing.

CHAPTER 52:

Foster Care Reformation Issue Continued

There was also a black male resident named Kenneth Barkley, who was pronounced dead because of a violent restraint at the Berea Children's Home I was at two years after I had left and my sister's homicide trial had wrapped. The battle to maintain our foster youth still rages on.

To the reader, you are the voice of the precious young life at the mercy of a rigid system. Even by you reading my story, the proceeds of this novel are going to help these vulnerable and impressionable young children who need an eye and a heart like yours to pioneer for them the most. Faith Forever Ministries. I started this ministry in homage to my twin sister and in supportive local art therapy services that promote our youth indulging in positive and healing activities for a vitally important cause. Yet the fight for the children of foster care's prosperity and protection cannot be fought alone! We are more powerful together. If you are out there still fighting, Faith Forever Ministries is here with you. Let us support one another on this journey called life and lean on God to strengthen us along the way.

In my experience, it is only Jesus' Holy Spirit entering our souls that can return us back to His perfect image of us. That image being offering an agape, or sacrificial kind of love, even to those who are strangers to us. Embracing God's love for all of humanity will enable us to love others who don't look, think, or believe in the same way that we do. The alternative is a life without Christ and the Holy Spirit anchoring our minds; we all truly become feral, wild animals at heart. Add the satanic influence of Satan's rebellious curse coming in to distort and destroy God's perfect image, and what you are left with is a loveless society only built on policing rules and refusing to embrace people that you decide are inferior. With the Holy Ghost, one can literally transform from a ravenous wolf-dog that can only be loyal to their kind into a domesticated mammal capable of befriending all different kinds of animals like cats, sheep, fish, birds, and more! We're all on Noah's ark together... for now. Let us always remember that we are more alike than we are not.

Notable Mentions of the Impact That Faith's Life Had on Others

Faith Nicole Finley, this weekend marks seven years since you quite literally saved my life in an attack that was meant to end it. I don't have much memory of the brutal assault besides knowing in my heart I was going to die. My only clear memory is watching that metal bar coming for my head but never feeling its blow. It would be upon regaining conscious-ness that I would learn you stopped it before it hit. You had tackled my would-be killer and held her down with all your might until the staff that was supposed to be protecting us finally got there. Had my life been dependent upon them doing their jobs, I'd be dead. I was covered in giant purple and black bruises on my forehead, cheek, entire back, legs, abdomen, and chest. Some were as big as basketballs. Somehow, I escaped without a single broken bone. Everything I have now; my husband, my beautiful children, my world, I owe in a big part to you.

Thirteen short hours later, you were murdered by the very staff members who had failed to do their jobs and intervene in my assault. For saving my life, yours was taken. Seven years later, we still do not have justice for your murder. I do not understand how that can happen in the world we live in. Thirteen hours before your life ended, you saved mine. I will forever and ever be grateful to have called you my friend, roommate, and hero.

I love you so much. I miss your dear smile, which was always so bright and pink from that lipstick I got for you on pass. I miss your kindness as you would stay up until 3 a.m. with me, doing devotionals and talking way past curfew. I'll never forget you nor take advantage of the gift you gave me. Fly high angel!

As the world is taking notice and people are rising up, there is another name that begs not to be forgotten. It's one you've never heard but deserves to be shouted from the rooftops.

This is her. She was a beautiful, loving black woman named Faith Nicole Finley.

On December 13th, 2008, I was attacked in foster care and beaten by another girl with a metal pipe off of an industrial broom. I was hit with the pipe over thirty times all over my head, back, neck, chest, legs, and hands and knocked into unconsciousness. My insulin pump was ripped so violently from my stomach that skin came with it, and my pump was smashed. I had clumps of hair torn out at the root. I was being actively beaten to death. Before that could happen, Faith intervened. She tore the girl off of me, took the pipe from her, held the girl down, and screamed for help until the people in authority who were supposed to be protecting us came. She confronted the people in positions of authority over their failures to protect me. They did not apologize, they did not care, and they blamed Faith for her anger. They fought her, held her down on the concrete floor, sat on her, and suffocated her. Three women, all much bigger than her tiny frame, made sure she couldn't breathe or move. She died there in one of the worst ways possible. She choked to death on her own vomit as they held her in place.

The last words I heard her speak were "I can't breathe." They laughed and said that if she could talk, she could breathe. They were wrong. She couldn't breathe. She couldn't breathe. She told them. She couldn't breathe.

This beautiful, vivacious black woman was murdered because she saved the life of a white girl — me.

The media would later crucify her as an emotionally unstable, silly little girl who had a tantrum. They didn't report my assault; they didn't report her intervening. They said she had a tantrum and was throwing things, so she was restrained. She wasn't having a tantrum. She was terrified, and she had just had to save my life. She was upset by their failures. She confronted authority. She demanded authority do better. At that moment, she wasn't a seventeen-year-old; she was an adult far beyond her years demanding the same thing all of these protests are demanding- action by authority.

In the months following, the three women who murdered Faith were brought before a judge. I was not allowed to be there. I was not allowed to testify to tell my story. What happened to me was never even mentioned. I was an "unreliable witness" because I was being treated for depression and suicidal ideation. I was forced into silence and held back legally from talking to anyone about what happened. Her family did not even know about me. Not until much later when I sought them out. This post is the most I've ever said. All three women walked, and they are free today; they never *served a day being named as murderers. They walk around living their lives, and Faith lies in a cemetery.*

If I face repercussions from this post, so be it. I will no longer be silent because my silence is complicity in a world that is suffocating and shooting and viciously ripping apart black men and women for being black and wanting more. Faith's death is a story that has been repeated and repeated and repeated. It happened long before she died, and it happens every day now. In every story I see, I see Faith before my eyes again. I see her on that concrete floor, begging to breathe. She couldn't breathe!

As you protest and say their names, say Faith Finley. Write it down, scream it out, hold it high on signs, and put it on shirts. Faith Finley.

#FaithFinley
#SayHerName
#FaithForeverMinistries
#GeorgeFloyd
#EricGarner
#IcantBreathe
#DemandMore
#Corruption
#BlackLivesMatter

View Faith's legacy and see her change the world for foster kids at Faith Forever Ministries. This organization is run by Faith's twin sister, Jordan Noellé Finley.

Please share Faith. Have people see her face and hear her name. She needs to be included in this conversation, and people need to know her like I knew her. A beautiful, loving woman, a hero, willing to jump into danger to save the life of a friend.

The girl who nearly killed me was white.

The girl who saved me was black.

The white girl was only ever restrained by the black girl. The staff never touched the white girl. They just ushered her out of the room. The one who was restrained was the hero, the black girl.

The person who assaulted me was charged and convicted of a felony.

The people who murdered Faith walk free.

No one can ever tell me Faith's death wasn't about race.

— Margaret Ellen Bradford

Excerpt from Judge Jill Flagg Lanzinger's recount of the Faith Finley case:

Remembering Faith Finley in 2014, who would be twenty-three years old today. Faith was a smart, sweet, artistic girl who shared her faith in God with struggling youths. As a direct result of Faith's death, the dangerous, prone position restraint was made illegal. Faith's death prevented the deaths and serious injuries of many other people in Ohio. A beautiful part of her still remains on this earth — happy birthday to her twin sister, Jordan Noellé Finley.

CHAPTER 54:

Poetry about Life in Prejudice Wooster and Kent

Too Black for the White Kids, Too White for the Black

The school bell's blaring ring reverberates in my ears as I hasten down my high school halls; this is the third time this month that my most recent "best friend," Ashley, has had something "come up" and couldn't meet me for lunch. To spare myself the lunchroom seating anxiety, I escape into an empty classroom safe from the eagerly judging eyes of my peers and relish in the respite. In a predominantly white school, I stand out enough as one of the few browns without drawing more attention to myself. This has been a recurring theme that has been happening ever since fifth grade when my best friend Rachel told me that she couldn't go biking with me after school because she had to study the Torah… only to later ride by and see her laughing and surrounded by a group of admiring boys at the local pool.

Hurry, I think to myself, *before the school bell rings and exposes you as factionless to the herd. They are all safely nestled in their packs, ready to devour you, lonely little wolf.*

How wondrously aloof it must feel to not have to worry about where you'll sit at lunch or who you'll sit with. Being one of the few brown kids at school makes a monumental achievement out of attaining simple comradery. The recurring theme of rejection shrouded in the convenience of coincidence looms over me and follows me around, relentlessly like a dark vapor, as I quietly slip into my last classroom of the day, so early that I'm only greeted by the silent hum of the teacher's projector. I have successfully evaded the detection of embarrassment that plagues the other fringe kids with social taunts and torment, yet from myself, the inner ridicule never elapses. The dark cloud still haunts me.

Memories flood in of the black girls at my last school riddling me with insults, "Why you talk white, you think you special 'cos you call people uncouth?"

Apparently, I act "too white" for the black kids, and I'm too black to blend in with the white. Too bad for you, lonely little wolf; you have no real friends that will stick by your side.

At dinner, my mom attempts to console me, saying, "Oh, it'll get better when you get to college. You know the smart kids are always objectified."

Easy for her to say, I think to myself, it's not like she went to school with a cellphone or had to care about having a "social media presence" on Twitter and Facebook. She may have had her own struggles, too, but her generation did not live in the same world as mine... those websites for friends to connect with one another have become weaponized for bullies to surreptitiously have access to endlessly terrorize... .

It's not "Oh woe is me" or a loud cry for pity, but rather a plea for some accountability. Someone, please be wary of the invisible acid that seeps into my chest each time I watch hypocrisy cause my friendships to die. Is it so childishly pitiful to envision myself as one of those glowing girls, laughing carefree with real comradery by her side?

The basketball my cousin dribbles beats jubilantly as his words hit me. *Plick, plack, plack!* "Oh, I forgot 'yo proper jerk always actin' white. Always worried about somebody being a Christian, straight cornball man. Hahaha. You wack."

I notice when we visit our family down South that my mother's scholarly diction lapses around my aunts and them; she even joins in on the teasing banter, just to spare herself the verbal jabs. "Keep getting attitude 'cos I told you to stop bringin' home Cs in math. Don't make me get a belt from ya uncle and beat your little jerk."

Ugh, what a coward, I think to myself.

My cousin interjects, "Aye, Auntie, funny man, hahah. She put you on blast!"

So much for "objectification," right, Mom? I roll my eyes and nod as I exit the kitchen; I'll come back when she's done with her Ebonics act.

When you're not even safe to be yourself at home, what's the use of even trying?

If liking to read poetry more than gossip rags makes me "lame" to the cool kids, then so be it; I'd rather have knowledge than illiteracy and material possessions controlling my brain, ruling my self-esteem.

Slurring my words to garner street cred only affords me temporary cool points. I can't keep it up; it always subsides. So, what's the use of even trying to hide?

I should act for acceptance because I am too white for the black kids and too black for the white kids, right?

No. I am too cultured for the inane, too passionate to ever be too heartless, shallow, haughty, and filled with self-pride, and for my true inner self, my identity, I will never compromise.

For She Has Holy Fire in Her Veins

For she has holy fire in her veins.

Do you ever sit and ponder our ancestors? Wonder how they survived those harrowing voyages on the unruly open sea or the rugged, wild western terrains?

It seems unfathomable that people lived without electricity or roads that paved the way.

What fueled the young Prairie girl and the southern sharecropping child to be able to lead oxen to plow grounds for miles? To work tirelessly in the fields raising animals, growing fruit, vegetables, and fresh whole grains?

It had to be the holy fire running in her veins.

That holy fire must be hereditary and passed down from generation to generation.

What makes me ponder on the pioneering woman's strength from yesterday?

If only we could somehow encapsulate their power and inject their strength into the women of this day and age.

The courage of Rosa Parks' steadfastness and the brawns of Laura Ingalls Wilder need to be implanted into the women of today so that their holy fire can ignite the causes we fought for from slipping into obscurity.

That vivaciousness that once compelled suffragists with absolutely no legal rights to boldly and eloquently write out their pleas for equality and today's popular culture is simply not there.

Today, it's considered "empowering" for a woman to opt for vulgar self-expression and to expose her body in provocative wear.

No one is suggesting that women in the twenty-first century live as if they were in the Victorian era in order to exude dignity.

Yet rather to uphold the intellectualism that the Trail Blazers before us fought for in the first, second, and third wave of women's liberation, a cause that women are still fighting for to this day.

The image of a woman bearing her breasts in the heyday of the 1970s was a supremely liberating portrayal of the dominant freedom that women possess over their sexuality, bodies, and lives. Whereas a decade prior, a woman needed her husband's written permission to even procure employment, this was an astonishing achievement.

The holiness is missing from modern day feminism today for women. Sexual freedom is only as liberating to the woman as a woman is liberated financially.

For example, if the same seductive and sultry lyrics were sung by a destitute woman living at the haven of rest versus a rich woman driving in a Bentley, the entire meaning is night and day and now becomes toxic. The song is only an anthem of empowerment if the woman is considered wealthy, which sends a message that only a rich woman can be sexually freed, and the poor woman can't participate as she will be viewed as promoting prostitution, an archaic regression to female slavery.

If the song cannot be sung by and empower all women of every race, age, and demographic, feminism falls flat and caters to misogynistic attitudes cloaked in women's liberty.

So, what inspires the modern-day feminist to stare down the sexually explicit culture and brand of femininity?

To challenge and expose its own hypocrisy directly in its face?

It is she who does not forget the lessons that she learned from her predecessors before her; it is she who finds a rising confidence in herself, knowing that she walks with the strength of her ancestors within her, for she has holy fire in her veins.

A Black Girl's Healing:
From Broken to Blessed

"Dear God, You are awesome!"

I hear the choir joyfully cheer.

How I long to one day fully feel the euphoria that they
feel.

A part of my heart burns with rage when I try to praise
You,

Because You know that I've been called to live out a
very hard life…

Even while I've prayed to You.

I prayed to You, God, as a young child,

"Lord, save my family from divorce; keep their marriage
alive! I need You to spare me of some of this pain…"

How can I really stand in church and sing "You are
awesome" with sincerity when inside I grapple with
if those prayers were done in vain?

Dear God, You are awesome.

Which is why I've been praying for you to heal me out
of my despair now for many years…

It doesn't matter if I scream in church or in the streets,
way up in the clouds; not like You'll ever hear.

What can I hope to gain in the world if I really sold it
my soul?

A nice house, a newer car, and even some

"Real" friends who would surely never fold.

The allure of wealth everlasting would

Buy their allegiance and seemingly give me what my
     flesh tells me You have not,
A support system unbuilt on sand and
Instead, on solid rock.

Dear God, I genuinely want to believe You are
     awesome.
With every fiber of my being.
Sometimes, the pessimist in me and
The cruelty of the world gets in the way…
I hope that You know that I'm really doing my best to
     believe and trust that You love me every day.
That with faith, the universe will open up to me,
Because I know that You give me the peace that passes
     all understanding.
For so many days, I wanted to leave this earth in
     exchange for eternity.
Through adversity, I have come to learn that even hard-
     ships themselves are a gift.
What a glorious attribute to those who have gone on
     before us and glory over every adversity.
The fact that You think that I am strong enough to
     survive these trials says something spiritual about
     You and about me.

Dear God, I do not understand Your mysterious ways,
Yet the ever-present seed of hope You've implanted in
     my soul pulsates deeper,
Hope whispers to my core that You hear me when I
     pray.

PHOTOS

Jordan Noellé Finley
Apr 12, 2012 · 🕐 · 🔒

faith in her room,she wrote 'faith and jordan's place' on the lil board behind her cos we shared the room.she was so beautiful, i wonder what she'd look like now that we're 20 and my face has matured so much.i love you faithy.

👍 You, Faith Nicole Finley and 41 others   11 comments

👍 Like   💬 Comment   ↪ Share

Jordan Noellé Finley at Jerusalem, Israel
Jan 3, 2012 · 🌐

My mom & I tried to take a picture outside... See more

Margaret Ellen Bradford with Faith Nicole Finley and Jordan Noelle Finley

December 9, 2015

Faith Nicole Finley this weekend marks 7 years since you quite literally saved my life in an attack that was meant to end it. I don't have much memory of the brutal assault besides knowing in my heart I was going to die. My only clear memory is watching that metal bar coming for my head but never feeling it's blow. It would be upon regaining consciousness that would learn you stopped it before it hit. You had tackled my would-be killer, and held her down with all your might until the staff that was supposed to be protecting us finally got there. Had my life been dependent upon them doing their jobs, I'd be dead. I was covered in gian purple and black bruises on my forehead, cheek, my entire back, legs, abdomen and chest. Some were as big as basketballs. Somehow I escaped without a single broken bone. Everything I have now, my husband, my beautiful children, my world, I owe in a big part to you

13 short hours later, you were murdered by the very staff members who had failed to do their jobs and intervene in my assault. For saving my life, yours was taken. 7 years later and we still do not have justice for your murder. I do not understand how that can happen in the world we live. 13 hours before your life ended, you saved mine. I will forever and ever be grateful to have called you my friend, roommate, and hero

I love you so much. I miss your dear smile, which as always so bright and pink from that lipstick I got for you on pass. I miss your kindness as you would stay up until 3AM with me doing devotionals and talking way past curfew. I'll never forget you nor take advantage of the gift you gave me. Fly high angel! 💜

" She was a heroine, a daughter, a twin, a lover, a friend, a protector, a Jesus advocate, a **legend.** "

34   11 Com

👍 Like   💬 Comment   ↪ Share

#SayHerName
#FaithFinleyForever

FaithFinleyFor

Striving to raise awareness for socia
creating a better society

14 sold

Help us reach our goal. If the fund is successful,
14 customers days after this fund ends on Jan 18.

Buy a Shirt

Unisex $12.00   Ladies $15.00   Long Sleeve $18.00   Sweatshirt $40.00

ALL PROCEEDS BENEFIT
FaithFinleyForeverMinistries
https://www.facebook.com/faithfi...

March 11, 2008

Dear God, well I know I was supposed to do this in the morning but I procrastinated all day for even getting up that Jordan had to drag me out of bed! Lol So you know – well I was interrupted but you already know what happened I just pray you help me tomorrow finish my book with understanding and I hope that it sticks with me. Well anyways thanks for blessing us.

Love,

[multiple signatures] Vera, Jennifer Lopez, Josephine, Princess Princess, Rihanna, Jennifer Love Hewitt, Faith, Mila Kunis, Jasmine Brown, Carina, Macy, Jacqueline, Paisley, Japo Finley, Paula, Janet Jackson, Jessica, Marilyn Monroe, Brandy, Norma Finley, Jessica Simpson, Jolene, Amanda Bynes

March 27, 2008

Dear Lord,

So fast-forward to Easter.
Which was the 23rd. We had a late
start because of Mommy being sick.
(But we were dressed up and ready).
We waited patiently Jordan wrote
to the girls in Juvie. I did little nothings
on myspace. She got ready finally.
We took pics and left. It was a nice
spring day. We were supposedly going
to a Chinese restaurant but it was
closed. So, after long deliberating we
decided on Red Lobster. Yea it's not
exactly the fanciest place ever but it
was nice enough. We played word games,
ate, took a few pictures, had fun, recognized
a guy from a old church. Then she wanted
to see The Other Boelyn Girl but we
really wanted to see There Will Be Blood.
So, she reluctantly agreed to see it.
So we bought time at Barnes & Nobles.
She had originally wanted to go to this
church service at a church we'd never
been to but we didn't. We saw There
Will Be Blood it was great! - she hated
it. She said it was boring, no dialog

because she was too crazy for Safe Landing.
She went to Childrens. I was I guess in shock
that she would do this all over again.
 But, later on I realized that Jordan and me
have lived half our lives under constant
stress about where we would live, food,
money etc. So, that and losing loved ones
that you can never get back so it's just
a lot of stress and depression (and also
me putting her through hell when we were
isolated and miserable) so all that built
up anger and stress finally let out. She's
been through counseling at Childrens
hospital. I saw her yesterday (she's normal
again. Thank you Jesus!) and should be
here soon. So, I still have stress and
masterbating is the only release I can get
nowadays. My only joy or strength or
anything. Personal counselors are coming
Saturday for me and Jordan. Betty our youth
group leader came (with Mcdonald's the
day before yesterday) to help and comfort me.
So, hopefully I can get some counseling too
so I can deal with my annoying insane
Mother who likes to call me a Bitch if I say
to unplug GFCI (because that's...

she started all that drama that night saying really mean things to her and disrespectful and appalling things that I never thought she would EVER say. So as you know Mommy called the cops, they came. Took Jordan to Juvie and the next day I had to go to court with Mommy. It was weird I was tired angry, and upset and trying to keep Mommy strong because if I was weak then she'd definitely fall apart because she's already so fragile as it is. Jordan came in some weird outfit with shackles (in court) and her chair a mess and I was shocked stunned... and everything Long story short she ended up staying again because I didn't think she was ready to come home because she didn't even seem appreciative and I believed Mommy's story about what happened because Jordan was so obviously out of control So, she came home a day later

March 26, 2008

Dear Lord,

Well I'm writing this in reprence to yesterday because I hadn't written you. Well, yesterday was okay except for me yelling but I was only trying to be heard because she (mom) never lets me get a word in. Ha, I apologized and all she said was "ok." I always forgive her so... whatever anyway I was mad at Jordan that day because I thought she was making up all her problems. Because as you know on the 19th she started this big, long feud w/ Mommy. Mommy claimed Jordan "punched" her but even though I didn't see it it didn't sound like Jordan had hit her at all. Also, when she was holding her down on the couch she said Jordan was "kicking" her in the back" when what I saw was Jordan's legs (in front of her own body) and her squirming away. Also, I was mad at her because

New Jerusalem Fellowship Church
2555 Palmyra S.W.
Warren, OH 44485

Pastor Neil Heller, Officiating
Pastor Ernest Walker, Officiating

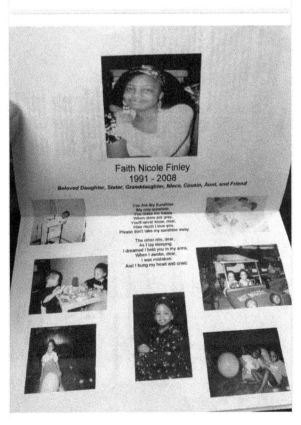

Faith Nicole Finley
1991 - 2008
Beloved Daughter, Sister, Granddaughter, Niece, Cousin, Aunt, and Friend

You Are My Sunshine
My only sunshine,
You make me happy
When skies are grey,
You'll never know, dear,
How much I love you,
Please don't take my sunshine away

The other nite, dear,
As I lay sleeping,
I dreamed I held you in my arms,
When I awoke, dear,
I was mistaken
And I hung my head and cried.

Printed in the USA
CPSIA information can be obtained
at www.ICGtesting.com
LVHW021403190924
791543LV00001B/41